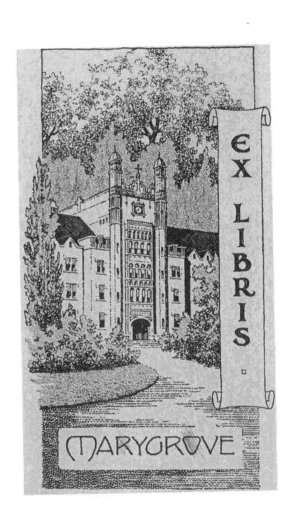

EX LIBRIS

MARYGROVE

CONTENTS

quotations or faithful adaptations and paraphrases of such speech and thoughts of her own as are recorded in letters, discourses, spiritual diaries and notes transmitted in the literature at my disposal.

I may therefore hope that my book, though not a biography in the sense of scholarly exactitude and completeness, may still serve its purpose, namely, to revive the memory of one of the most extraordinary women of the seventeenth century, indeed perhaps of the whole history of Religious Orders, and to re-tell, in a reliable, if romantic tale, the wonderful and enthralling adventure of her strangely tragic life.

IDA FRIED. GOERRES.

LEIPZIG,
ON THE FEAST OF THE NATIVITY
OF OUR LADY, 1938.

PART I

ONCE upon a time—thus begin all wonderful stories, even when they happen to be true.

God's storm-wind swept over the woods and moors of Northumberland. It raged among the oak-trees so that the dry leaves of last year's autumn rattled as they were whirled through the snow, the thick flakes enshrouding them before they reached the ground. Snow, snow, ever since Christmas, snow covering every track in the woods, and travellers freezing to death on the highways. Such weather had its bad, but also its good side; for it is an ill wind that blows no one any good. Bad, for it was now that hallowed season when priests were abroad in the land, secret and fugitive men, to-day, maybe, disguised as peasants, to-morrow as troopers in leather jerkins and round steel helmets, or as scholars in starched ruffs and black steeple-crowned hats ambling along to Oxford, or even as courtiers with wide-topped riding-boots, love-locks and little pointed beards. But in the depths of every man's baggage, hidden away under the apples and bacon for the market, Latin folios and scholar's gown, or velvet doublets and French gloves, were always the self-same things: chalice and paten, oil in pewter container, stole and relic for the altar. For a hero's tomb it must be whereon the sacred Body of Our Lord reposes when He descends to earth.

All around the lonely manors and farms where the mystery horsemen vanished into the night, there were strange unwonted activities. Lanterns bobbed up and down along hedges and ditches, bolts and bars were closely scrutinized and dogs posted on thresholds. Within doors, women were bustling about, like Martha, with shining eyes. There was a fragrance in the air as of waxen candles and fair linen from lavender-scented chests, and lads fingered the new hunting-knives purchased at last year's fair, their pulses quickening as they dreamt of betrayals, surprise attacks, and a hero's death. . . . "'Tis I who's the first to hear them when they come. . . . I make a rush for the door and keep them at bay, even if they strip me and hang me up over the hearth—I'll hold them back till the Father has had time to get away through the cellar and Mother has hidden the sacred vessels in the big butter-tub. Of course, in the end, they're bound to force their way into the hall, and then. . . ."

Thus the lads dreamt on, almost wishing in their hearts that it might be so, just as they'd heard folks tell; that would be something worth living for! And to them, it still seemed part of the dream, even when they found themselves actually in the hidden chamber, with the doors well bolted and barred, kneeling with the other children in their places at the back of the room, with father, mother and the other members of the household on the carpet in front, together with the faithful from the village, who appeared somehow to have got wind of what was going forward.

And there before the table spread with fresh linen and decked with sprigs of fir and scarlet berries, close to the hearth from which the trap-door led down to the cellar, stood the stranger-priest and blessed bread and wine and raised them aloft between the tall candles that gleamed like swords raised in a royal salute.

Every now and then, the silence was broken by the sobbing of the old folks. They were thinking back on her grandparents and felt not a little proud of the privilege.

One summer, when Mary was ten years old, another visitor arrived, to wit her own mother's youngest sister Martha Wright, who was but five years older than Mary herself. It was not long before the little girl had neither eyes nor ears for anyone else. Never in all her life had she seen anybody quite like her new aunt. She wore a jaunty little cap of green velvet adorned with a feather, and around her neck a very crisp starched ruff, whilst a small round mirror dangled from her waist, and occasionally the little girl was allowed to have a peep at herself in it. Aunt Martha had quite a collection of exciting little boxes of carved ivory and clouded glass and little silver bottles engraved with twisty-twirly letters that exhaled powerful and delicious fragrances. Grandmother was not allowed to know anything about these things, which were kept carefully hidden away in a brown leather valise, the old lady on the very first night of her daughter's arrival having expressed some very outspoken sentiments on the subject of certain silly and heathenish vanities which had no place in a Christian house.

All the same, she refrained from bearing too tight a hand on this daughter of hers; for, after all, she was already betrothed and was to be married the following spring. Martha, too, had been sent to this remote little manor-house to be kept out of harm's way, but also with the idea of giving her an opportunity to perfect herself in housewifely accomplishments. It thus happened that the two girls were thrown a good deal together, and Mary pricked both her sharp little ears when her aunt began to discourse on the strange and marvellously excit-

ing things that went on in a world where the forbidden
fineries, which now could be taken out and stroked and
admired only by candlelight, were just everyday things.
Mary heard a good deal about the great Queen Elizabeth,
who lived in London, and whose name she had never
heard mentioned at table without her grandparents
making the sign of the cross. But surely, Mary demurred,
she was the same wicked woman who had good pious
folk thrown into prison and deprived of all they possessed,
and who had priests hunted like wild beasts the length
and the breadth of the land. She had always pictured her
like the witches in the fairy stories, old and hideous,
with one enormous cruel fang, matted hair, and a club
foot protruding from the hem of her ragged gown.
"Oh, you little goose!" cried Martha. "Why, the Queen
claims to be the fairest woman in all the land; the youngest
and handsomest knights and gentlemen are enlisted in
her service, and they serve her with a right good will. . . .
They say that a glance from her eyes can bewitch a man
to such an extent that his life becomes to him a thing
of little account so he can perform deeds of superhuman
valour for her sake. . . . They call her Gloriana, like
the fairy queen; she wears pearls on her shoes, and her
hair flames red like the sun, and in her wardrobes she
has three thousand silk and velvet dresses. All the princes
and rulers of the world have sought her hand in marriage,
but she will have none of them, nor will she share
her throne with any man, for she is resolved to rule alone.
. . . And you mean to say that you have never heard
anything of all this?"

"No, never," Mary was obliged to own, feeling intensely ashamed of her ignorance and exceedingly young
and foolish. Nor had she heard of the glorious Armada
and its inglorious end off Plymouth one sultry night in

July but seven years ago. . . . "But you were not even able to toddle then, you funny little thing, you. . . . She's like Judith in the Bible, like Esther, and that wicked Queen Jezebel all put together." After that Mary perused the Scriptures with unprecedented zeal, visualizing everything she read against the glamorous background of the English court.

Sometimes when they sat all alone in the lofty narrow room where the linen was stored, and the tiny stitches in the work they were doing began to blur in the gathering twilight, Martha would suddenly drop her hem, stretch herself and cry: "Oh, how mortally tedious it all is! Come, let's have a dance!" And Mary, infected with something of the elder girl's vivacious high spirits, would then rise timidly to her feet, allow the other to take her by the hand and show her her steps, and in this way the two girls practised untiringly the Coronato, Lavolta and the formal Peacock Dance, Martha softly whistling the musical accompaniment the while.

But she knew a great many other things, that wonderful kinswoman of hers. She was already betrothed. Her future husband's name was Thomas Percy, and he was a cousin of the Earl of Northumberland: one day he would rank high in the land, for even now he was far cleverer, more accomplished, more courtly, and more courageous than any of his peers. She had letters from him, too, penned with wondrous flourishes of superlative elegance; also equally elegant poems, which she read to her little cousin of nights; the latter understood nothing at all of the sonnets, but it was all delightfully mysterious and unreal.

Martha had brought her own maid along with her; her name was Meg, and she had insolent little black eyes. Grandmother did not approve of the girls associat-

ing with the servants, so at meals Meg sat, sullen, albeit
somewhat subdued, amongst the stiff old serving-maids,
who regarded her with a disapproval they were at no
pains to disguise, reminding Mary somehow of a mag-
pie amidst an assembly of crows. But, at nightfall,
there would come a tap at the window of the room
where the two girls, despite the rule forbidding any
talking after night prayers, were sitting up in bed with
their arms slung about one another, waiting for the
signal. Martha would then open the window very,
very softly and Meg crept in like a little black cat. After
that there was always a good deal of excited whispering
and giggling between the two grown-ups, Mary not
always being allowed to listen. Or the big valise with all
the forbidden fineries was dragged out of the wardrobe,
and Martha donned the costly new-fangled garments that
she was not allowed to wear at Ploughland. Then she
would trip up and down the room with mincing steps
and ridiculous airs and graces, making faces and imitating
various people she knew, until she was obliged to fling
herself on the bed to smother peal after peal of laughter,
whilst the little girl, with her finger in her mouth,
squatted on the pillows, lost in solemn wonder.

One night, Meg arrived, bursting with excitement,
and announced that she had discovered a fortune-teller
in the village, a real live witch, all complete with a
crystal globe. What fun it would be to have their fortunes told! After many secret palavers, the three young
things climbed out of a ground-floor window that
opened on to the neglected garden, sped swiftly, shoes
in hand, through the cool grass and a night heavy with
the perfume of elder blossom and, much to their dis-
comfiture, bright with the greenish light of a summer
moon, clambered over the crumbling old garden wall

and, quivering with excitement, entered the red brick cottage where the witch lived by the mill-race. The roaring of the water and the noise of the mill-wheel, which sounded louder than ever in the stillness of the night, drowned the creaking of the door as they entered and closed it behind them.

In a spotlessly clean little room, on a footstool beside the empty hearth, over which strings of strong-smelling herbs were hung up to dry, sat an old woman in a russet gown relieved with a white kerchief. She was smoking a short pipe, and in the blue haze that pervaded the tiny room, the cat humping its back on the hearth seemed to bristle up to more than life-size. Mary stared around her lost in amazement. She would not have been one whit surprised if the animal had begun to talk or the enormous pumpkin she could just make out in a dark corner had been transformed before her very eyes into Cinderella's coach. But nothing happened. The old woman was mumbling something through her discoloured teeth, and Mary pricked her ears when she heard the words: "Everything's ready, my lovelies, everything's ready for seeing what the future has for you in store."

Then they all sat down in a row, Mary very pale, the others very red. The old woman laid aside her pipe, placed on the table a large crystal globe with a curious kind of pedestal and, with strange dead eyes, gazed fixedly at the gleaming ball, her hands stretched out, and her fingers clawing the air, as though she would conjure spirits from the deep. Mary only half caught the drift of what she was muttering to the other two, but there seemed to be a great number of gentlemen involved, as well as gold, curses, vengeance, and tears. Martha sat there looking frankly scared, whilst Meg tried to laugh it all off in her usual insolent way. Then Mary's turn came.

The old woman groaned and wheezed and rolled her big head, her fingers clawing and writhing in the smoky blue air that seemed to curdle the very moonlight as it streamed into the room. "You'll cross the sea," she said, "a long, long journey . . . oh, I can't see properly . . . it's all gone blurred again. . . . Cities, strange cities . . . it's not England . . . I don't know where it is."

Then, after a long oppressive silence: "There are mountains, high mountains, all covered with snow. . . . You're walking along behind a mule, and you're wearing a big black hat, like the women of Cornwall wear. . . . You're very pale . . . you're limping. . . . Now you're standing in a big room with a great many men in scarlet cloaks seated around you. . . . Now I see a small dark room with a graveyard outside. . . ."

Martha uttered a piercing scream. She had suddenly lost her last vestige of self-control and was trembling with fear. She pushed the crystal into the old woman's lap, who, gasping as though she were at the point of death, collapsed in a heap, then she seized Meg by the arm and made a rush for the door. Breathlessly the girls raced home, exchanging never a word until, shivering with fear, they lay safe and sound again in their beds. Mary had an uncomfortable feeling that they had done something wrong. She felt annoyed with Martha and Meg, and even more with herself for her part in such an escapade. The next morning she flatly refused to lead the family prayers. She felt utterly miserable when the clear eyes that looked down on her from her beloved picture met her own, but her lips remained obstinately closed and she let her grandmother send her out

"Methinks, you're still hankering to be a Father as you used to do when you were five years old," he teased her in his good-natured way.

"But I'm only a girl," she said unsmilingly, then bit her lip hard, as though to stop the big angry tears that began to fall on the silk stretched across her embroidery-frame.

It was cruel of Daddy to make jokes like that. Couldn't he really guess what for so long had been her one long daydream? If I were a boy. . . . Only another three or four years. . . . I'd be learning Latin without anyone knowing the while. . . . Then, over the sea to St. Omer! The Jesuit College—a few short years more at the Seminary, then back again to England . . . an outcast and proscribed by the law of the land, but in secret a knight errant. . . . I know every inch of the ground, could risk any disguise—oh, they can set all their dogs at my heels, I'll warrant I'll give them the slip. . . . Anxious moments hidden behind some arras and listening whilst the soldiers search the rooms—long rides, with my reins a-dangling, beneath a starlit sky with the Venerabile safe beneath my cloak, close to my breast—burning, eloquent words in prison, till the feeble spark in every faltering soul again shoots heavenwards, straight as a flame. And then, the end: the cart to Tyburn . . . like Edmund Campion, holy, glorious, noble, martyred Edmund Campion—last words flung like torches amongst the people from the ladder that leads to the gallows, so that even before the blood-stained block, they fall on their knees. . . . And then—oh bitter, desolate awakening: I'm only a girl!

In the meantime, the wave of persecution sweeping over the land had swelled to a mighty sea. The prisons were filled to overflowing, whilst ever and anon the news passed fearfully from mouth to mouth that many priests had died the martyr's death, if it were not blazoned abroad with every revolting detail in countless broadsheets. And among the victims there were always many familiar names.

One day saddlebags and coffers were hastily packed for yet another exodus, and by coach or on horseback the entire family took the road for the north. Then came the parting of the ways, and Mary was consigned to the care of Mistress Ardington at Harewell.

Blurred and swiftly the days slipped past, those last warm days of a dying summer beneath the apple-trees bowed beneath the burden of their ripening fruit. Mary saw and heard but little of what was going on around her, for one thought alone suffused her whole being with a gentle glow. On Our Lady's birthday she was to receive her Lord for the first time. Only then did she feel that in very truth she would be one with those who like a living wall—battered and bloodstained, alas, but still unyielding—defended His sacred banner with their very lives. . . .

Lowering twilight hung over the cornfields; from the gathering gloom the cry of the cricket shrilled like a note of fear and tiny chill gusts of wind stirred eerily amongst the flowers. Mary knelt in the chapel. Any day now the priest might be expected of whose coming they had had secret notice and who was to stay over the feast at Harewell. The narrow window stood open, rattling every now and then against the wall of the chapel with a vaguely disquieting sound. Moths flew blindly in, dark nightborn creatures on silent wings.

Surely that was a whistle she heard from somewhere outside? Every sound carried so distinctly in the dead stillness of that Sabbath eve. Then suddenly it seemed

to her that someone was calling, some inner voice, calling
her without a sound, and she knew beyond any possibility
of doubt that somebody was waiting for her outside.

Already from the threshold she could just make out
the silhouette of a horseman at the entrance gate. And
yet, she mused, I heard no sound of horse's hoofs. . . .
In the warm blue-green twilight she could see that the
stranger was holding out to her a sealed letter, which,
he said, was from her father and which was to be read
at once. Neither the horseman's face nor voice was
familiar to her, and he was certainly not one of her
father's men, so she felt all the more perplexed when he
said that he had orders not to allow the letter to pass out
of his hands so would have to read it to her. . . .

"By my blessing, I command you, my beloved daughter,
to abandon forthwith your preparation for receiving the
Sacrament and to return home. We have a most excellent
and suitable alliance in view for you. . . ."

Before Mary had time to reply or to ask a single
question, the horseman doffed his hat with a flourish
and vanished into the sombre green of the gathering
shadows as silently as he had come. The summer lightning playing more and more fitfully over the white
highroad revealed not a trace of any human form.

The girl was conscious of a sudden chill of fear and she
hurried back to the house which seemed to receive her
like the shelter of a protecting embrace. The widow
Ardington said very little when she heard the strange
story; she had been sitting at the window, and yet
had seen nothing of what had passed. . . . She crossed
herself and the child repeatedly with holy water, then,
armed with a branch from the Garden of Gethsemane in
Jerusalem, a family heirloom of some long-distant

pilgrimage, she went the round of all the rooms of the house, laying the leaves of blessed herbs on all the beds. And that night they both recited the Ninetieth Psalm aloud and very earnestly three times in succession. Another letter, this time from Mistress Ardington, went speeding to the north, and when Sir Marmaduke's reply arrived saying that no messenger had been sent by him and that most certainly Mary could count on his blessing for the greatest day of her life, they exchanged silent, but very meaning looks, and that night the Ninetieth Psalm was again recited as before. For, from the very first, they had not had the slightest doubt as to the true identity of the mysterious horseman.

Being sixteen is much worse than being thirteen. Have Mother and Father grown so very different, Mary asked herself, or is it only I? To think that even Father, best and most understanding of fathers, simply cannot grasp that I mean what I say and that I don't want to hear another word on the subject of marriage nor the eternal talk about suitors and good and wealthy matches and desirable husbands. . . . After all, Elizabeth and Barbara are still there, why must it always be I? It's enough to make one sick or run away from home, when every few weeks when bedtime comes and the candles are brought in, one of my parents—it's usually poor little mother who musters up courage to have another try—takes one gently by the hand, puts on a solemn look and begins in a hushed voice, as though they were breaking the news of somebody's death: "My child, I want to have a serious talk with you. . . ." Then you have to sit down by the fire with your heart sinking in your shoes before they've even started. . . .

Oh, those noble, high-born youths, how heartily she

wished them to the uttermost ends of the earth, so heartily, in fact, that at her nightly examination of conscience, she would occasionally ask herself whether such feelings were quite compatible with the virtue of Christian charity. . . . All the same, it was very trying for a girl when young gentlemen were continually arriving on a visit, and every time the whole ridiculous business started all over again. She knew the game already by heart. The first few days they'd be quite nice and sensible, very much like her own big brother, whom they were supposed to be visiting. A bit stolid they were, to be sure, those young squires and lordlings, and perhaps a bit over-fond of their food, also occasionally a trifle noisy over their beer after the ladies had retired. Apart from that, they were quite decent lads, bashful and yet rather too sure of their own importance and their powers. Their conversation was mainly about hunting and horses and fighting and conspiracies; they rapped out great oaths when they discussed the bad times, and were immediately struck dumb with horror on suddenly remembering that the ladies were present. They were fair or dark or red, and most of them had clear eyes like little boys and were as clumsy as unlicked cubs. No, they were not really so bad. Occasionally, too, there would be one or the other amongst them a little older than the rest, a serious, well-read man who had travelled abroad and would talk to her father of an evening of Holland, France, Germany or Sweden, so that she felt she could listen to him for hours. But "Part Two" was bound to follow in the end. They'd begin to gaze at her with hungry eyes, for all the world as though they were bear-cubs and she were the honey in the comb; they would get red in the face and stutter and stammer instead of giving her a plain answer to some perfectly simple question—how well she had got to know all the symptoms, and how absurd and hateful it all was! And the end was always the same—the usual "serious talk" with father or mother in the ingle-nook of an evening.

Recently her father had said, quite crossly too, that it was time she stopped giving herself such ridiculous airs; at sixteen a girl was getting on in life—or was she thinking, perhaps, of going into a convent?—A convent —what was that? She seemed to have some hazy recollection that in the old days, when Edward the Confessor was king, devout women did penance by having themselves immured, or something similar. She certainly would not dream of doing such a thing. Her father seemed quite mollified by this disdainful answer and supposed that it was merely poor Ralph Eldrington who had not been fortunate enough to find favour in the Princess's eyes; never mind, one of these days somebody would be found more to Her Highness's fastidious taste. . . .

After that, however, her mother began to din her day after day with Eldrington's praises, just as though matters could be improved by wasting a lot of words on the subject. Mary said nothing, but she began to lose her appetite and dark circles appeared around her eyes. Her sisters heard her at night sobbing and tossing about in her bed, and one day when she was folding the household linen, she suddenly and for no apparent reason, doubled up in a fainting-fit.

Moved with something very like remorse, Sir Marmaduke had a talk with his wife, who of late seemed to have shrunk and aged beneath the burden of all her worries. "You're both making yourselves ill," he said, "you as well

night has burst into bloom; she was radiant with the
dreamy entrancing beauty of a first-love. The others
often smiled, half amused and not a little wistfully, as
one smiles at young lovers who imagine that they have
a secret all to themselves and yet betray it with every
happy glance.

One night when Mary had again unobtrusively
slipped out of the room, Sir George said to Lady Grace:
"This winter, my lady mother, you can save your candles.
All you have to do is to post our young cousin in the
hall, and I warrant we shall have all the light we need
from her halo."

The others laughed, but Lady Grace chid them
gravely: "I trust none of you will upset the child with
your foolish jests. Sleep-walkers may roam the roofs
and high places without hurting a hair of their heads—
but only as long as nobody calls them by name."

To Mary the good lady showed a motherly indulgence,
making no comment when the girl absented herself
from their little family feasts, when she withdrew to her
sacristy as soon as a visitor was announced, raising no
protest when her mode of dress grew plainer and austerer
as the years went by, appearing blind to the fact that for
some long time past she had worn no jewels. Alas,
how little it was she could do! was Mary's own reflection. In the *Lives of the Saints* she had read so much
about mortification and bitterness of spirit. She had
also made some personal experiments in that direction
but with no conspicuous success. For it was sweet, not
bitter, when your limbs ached with chill fatigue; sweet
was the burning thirst of a hot summer when she
would deny herself a single drop to drink for days at
a time; sweet was the sapping, grinding hunger of fasting
—bitter alone was the hateful, miserable sense of degrada-

D

tion when again she had yielded to her craving and had eaten just a little more than was barely necessary . . . no, never would she have believed that a tiny morsel of rye bread could have stuck so abominably in one's throat.

The spiked girdle, too, that after much cudgelling of her brains she had managed to fashion with bits of wire and which she wore next her skin under her gown of coarse blue cloth, was, she felt, little better than a childish toy. For she was happy, so unspeakably, so blissfully happy, so what booted a few scratches or a patch or two of swollen, angry skin?

Sometimes she felt almost sad because her life had remained so singularly untouched by sorrow, because somehow she had failed to discover the royal road of the Cross, which after all was the road that all the Saints had trod. In what way had she made herself unworthy of God's favour and the seal of His friendship? Was she still too dependent on human love? Did she find more pleasure than she should in the kindness and indulgence of her kinsfolk, in the quiet deference and in the subtly intoxicating incense of their admiring awe? Had she not recently experienced a swift little thrill of pride when Sir Ralph, still immersed in his family papers, told them over dinner that he had discovered beyond any shadow of doubt that one of her ancestors, a Ward of Givendale, was already famous as a Warden of the Border ten years before the coming of the Conqueror? Alas, she was still puffed up with pride and worldly vanity.

When the next batch of visitors arrived from the surrounding manors, they found her with her sleeves tucked up, a handkerchief over her head, and a pail of water beside her, on her hands and knees scrubbing the stairs.

She was glad that they had honestly taken her for one of the maids, even more glad when Lady Arabella, on recognizing her, ordered her in an undertone, but with an unmistakable snap in it, to go and change her things at once, such foolish tricks being utterly beneath the dignity of a lady.

One day a scullery maid, her face and arms covered with a horrible eruption, came to Lady Grace who was skilled in all healing arts. Mary had to hold the pot of ointment and hand the strips of linen to her aunt, but a rising sense of nausea choked her and forced her to turn her head aside, whereas her aunt cheerfully joked away, rubbing in the ointment with a right good will and with never a sign of disgust.

For the rest of the day, Mary went about looking extremely pale and worried. That same night the sick girl was not a little startled to see Mistress Mary suddenly materialize beside her bed, white as any ghost, and to hear her command in a voice that sounded entirely strange: "You're not to say a single word now, and, on your soul, you're never to breathe a word to anybody that I've been here."

And she wriggled into the nasty stifling heat of the disordered bed, pressing her face close to the rough clammy cheek of the sick girl who, fidgeting and perspiring in her alarm and embarrassment, was quite unable to close an eye until the young lady, after some highly uncomfortable hours, finally rose and slipped away as quietly as she had come.

A few days later, Mary herself was going about looking like poor Lazarus in the Bible. However, when Lady Grace arrived with her pot of ointment, the look of dismay and piteous entreaty in the dark eyes that met her own was so eloquent that she hastily retired with her remedies, shaking her head and murmuring to herself with a sigh: "If only the Holy Ghost would inspire the girl to do something a bit more sensible for once in a way!"

She urged her niece to discuss her spiritual exercises with one of the priests who were continually visiting the house—Father Pollard had long departed, for Mary was now three years at Babthorpe—but the girl flushed crimson and stared at her in utter bewilderment. Discuss one's most intimate secrets with a stranger—nay, and even were he a persecuted confessor of the faith? Impossible! The sacrament of penance was bad enough as it was—even though one hadn't very much to say—but, of course, there was no getting over that. But over and above that—really, Aunt sometimes had the strangest ideas.

Then, one red-golden autumn evening, in the apple-loft, where they were setting out the fruit on the long, straw-covered shelves and sorting out the tainted ones, Mary made the amazing and unexpected discovery that old Margaret Garrett, who had part of the household under her charge, had lived in her childhood quite close to a convent. Her father had been gardener to the Cistercian nuns of Eshwold, and Margaret had been a constant visitor to the convent of the White Ladies. She had even wanted to enter the convent herself, but then came the great dissolution of the monasteries under King Henry, and the nuns had migrated to France.

Unforgettable winter and unforgettable evenings spent in the old lady's room, with its odour of baking apples and unbleached wool. Margaret Garrett sat at her spinning-wheel and the girls—for Barbara, the youngest of the Babthorpe daughters, a fair-haired, chubby eight-year-old, followed Mary about like her shadow—sat at her feet in the bay window on bright-coloured patch-work cushions, the little girl holding the wool which Mary wound to huge balls, whilst out of doors the snow whirled and eddied and the frost traced magic silvery ice-blossoms on the diamond panes and the thick soft cushion of snow on the window-sill outside crept higher and higher, white as the snowy coif on the old woman's head.

And Margaret Garrett would tell her story of once upon a time. She told of the tall grey convent church, of the nuns in their white habits behind the screen in the choir, of that long, sublime psalmody that began soon after midnight. Of course, she had not been allowed in the enclosure, but once—and after that on several other occasions—she had climbed up the ivy on the convent wall and had peeped into the garden. And there they were, the holy women, walking to and fro in their heavy white woollen habits, their hands tucked away in their sleeves and their eyes cast on the ground. They wore strips of white linen over their foreheads and black veils over their close-cropped heads, both by day and by night. They had to sleep in their clothes, like soldiers on a battlefield, ready at the first sound of the bell to rise and walk in a long line, two by two, to the church to sing the praises of God whilst the rest of the world lay sleeping. All around the garden were stone cloisters on slender twin columns, enclosed in winter by windows of stained glass. In summer red roses twined round the great cross in the centre of the square plot of grass, and encircling the fountain that gushed from a round basin at its foot, stood tall, gleaming white lilies. Sister Agatha at the wicket had been something of a chatterbox, but, then, she knew Margaret wanted to enter religion. So she counted her already almost as one of themselves, hoping it wasn't really wrong that she told her so much.

The nuns had their meals in a long hall with a vaulted ceiling and without any fireplace, and they ate at bare tables from wooden platters. The novices waited on them, even those of high degree—for noble, and even royal blood was nothing uncommon in the houses of St. Benedict and St. Bernard.

Once Sister Agatha was absent for three days from the wicket; a strange nun performed her duties and gave no answer when Margaret inquired with much concern whether her friend was ill. And when the latter returned to her post, she confided to the girl with many tears that as penance for having given the Prioress a pert answer, she had been excluded from both board and choir, that it had been like Purgatory to her, and that most certainly she would never repeat the offence. All the same, she was soon in trouble again for chattering too long at the wicket and arriving late for Vespers.

"What, for such a little thing!" cried Mary.

The old woman nodded her head impressively and said: "In a convent there's no such thing as little things. 'Tis a sublime and holy state and they who embrace it must be perfect in all things. Religious are the jewels of Holy Church, and a gem can be turned to good account only when it is quite without a flaw."

After that, Mary was silent.

*　　　*　　　*　　　*　　　*

A sublime and holy state. They who embrace it must be perfect. Was she really the same girl who four years ago had so violently protested when her father asked her whether she was thinking of entering a convent because she had refused to marry poor Eldrington?

Now she had another daydream, passionate, secret, without end, like the one she had had when she was fourteen years old and used to picture to herself the life of a gallant missionary. But that, of course, had been hopeless and really only make-believe, whereas beyond this other dream there was a faint gleam of hope, growing clearer and brighter with every succeeding day until it grew to a veritable agony of longing. She could never be a priest; God had assigned to her woman's lesser part—well and good. But if it were true that women could do good to none but themselves and to the others at best through their prayers—bitter, bitter indigence, but God willed that it should be thus!—then at least she would seek out the austerest order of them all, some day, and do that which was within her allotted scope with all her might and unremitting zeal.

Thenceforward, her little room was a cell pure and simple; her office was recited no longer as a purely voluntary act of devotion but under a solemn sense of obligation. She went about with lowered eyes and would have liked to tuck her hands inside her sleeves—it was a pity they were too tight at the wrist. By a happy chance, whilst helping Sir Ralph to bring his chaotic library into some sort of order, she came across an old conventual book of devotions entitled *A Golden Censer of Delicate Fragrance before the Face of the Most High*, and she tried with the most painstaking care all the marvellous recipes for devotion prescribed therein, all the gentle dalliance of conventual piety, such as placing every room in the house under the protection of its own particular saint, for whom you had a special devotion and whose example you tried to follow as long as you tarried within its walls. Or setting every day of the week aside for the practice of some different virtue and on Saturday winding them all, as it were, to a garland to lay at the feet of Our Lady. . . .

A missionary priest who heard her confession presented her with a little book entitled *The Spiritual Combat* by that venerable servant of God, Lorenzo Scupoli, a veritable treasure-store of spiritual wisdom. In this book her hungry soul found the sustenance for which it had been longing; she knew it practically by heart, carried it about with her wherever she went, tried to conform in every way to its precepts, from her resolution on waking till her final act of worship and contrition before she fell asleep. She practised that continuous form of prayer which is nothing else than walking always in the sight of God.

What did she reck that for some days past the chief topics of conversation amongst her kinsmen had been the Queen's sickness, the Scottish Stuart as probable successor, the problematic religious standpoint of Mary Stuart's son, and what changes were to be expected from the advent of the new sovereign. What concern were they of hers, those things they talked about in whispers: how the terrible old Queen lay propped up on a heap of pillows in the bedchamber of her palace of Whitehall, afraid to go to bed, hovering between life and death, eating nothing, uttering never a word, lolling there with her finger in her mouth and her glassy eyes fixed on the carpet. Mary had other things to think about, for ever since the feast of St. Thomas she had been preparing herself for her great account, for that general confession which, she had gleaned from her little book, was a highly commendable practice and eminently pleasing in the sight of God. One windy morning in March, shortly before Easter, as she knelt preparing herself in the chapel, where the first primroses shimmered pale yellow in their pots of moss on the altar, she heard the galloping of horse's hoofs beyond the park on the highroad that led to the north. It was Sir Robert Cary, speeding to Scotland with the tidings of the Queen's death. "And now, O ye kings, understand: receive instruction, you that judge the earth," the girl read in her psalms. "Thou shalt rule them with a rod of iron and shalt break them in pieces like a potter's vessel."

Without as much as a tremor of the eyelids, Mary closed her book, then rose from her place to light the candles for mass.

Later over breakfast, the priest, who had just returned from the Continent, was describing a visit he had paid to a famous French convent. In the very middle of a sentence, Mary rose from the table and hurried from the room, but not before the others had caught a glimpse of the tears that were streaming down her face.

"A pretty business this, Lady Grace," said the Father stroking his beard, "a pretty business."

"A pretty business forsooth!" the old lady repeated grimly. So grimly that Barbara gazed at her mother in open-mouthed astonishment.

That night Lady Grace had a long talk with her niece. "Everything within reason, child," she said gravely and firmly, "but such nonsense I absolutely refuse to countenance in my house. I have no wish to praise myself, but here at Babthorpe, as you very well know, we lead good Christian lives. I've always been glad that Our Lord thought fit to single you out for special favours

and have never stood in your way even when the
Holy Ghost did move you to do some very strange
things—nay, not even in that silly business with the itch.
But that you are now seriously thinking of going to
France and of entering a convent over there, that's nonsense, sheer foolishness, do you hear me?—Dear
heart, a pretty state of affairs it would be if, after we've
succeeded, in the face of innumerable difficulties, in rear-
ing our children for the Faith, they were to betake themselves off in our old age and leave us here in our misery!
You know, of course, that if you go, you'll be banished
and disinherited and will never be allowed to return?
Your parents have been at such infinite pains to give
their children a good Christian upbringing, and your
father has risked his life more than once to do so, so the
least you can do is to stand by him in these troublous
times. Old as I am, Mary, I would blush for very
shame to leave our sorely harassed Church here in her
extremity and go off to seclude myself in some comfortable foreign paradise."

And thus it went on for hours, whilst Mary sat there
beside her aunt looking very pale and miserable and
without opening her mouth to utter a word.

Then came the other relatives, the married daughters
of the house who, of course, long ago had also had
such foolish girlish fancies "until my eyes were opened
to the truly Christian vocation of wife and mother,"
the nice boy-cousins who talked about family and
honour and about holding out at one's post. Sir Ralph
was the only one who did not say much, but she often
caught him looking at her across the table with a worried
air of disapproval, and once he said to his wife: "I'm
glad she's no daughter of mine."

Mary suddenly found herself a stranger in the beloved

house. She went about her little duties and devotions just as usual, but there was a shadow brooding over everything, and the atmosphere was heavy with dim forebodings. Alas, that there was nobody, absolutely nobody to whom one could open one's heart! So her lips remained more tightly closed than ever and tiny hard lines began to appear round her mouth. One sultry afternoon whilst she was mending the household linen and the rain beat against the panes, flies seemed to be crawling everywhere, and the whole world looked indescribably grey and drear, she suddenly began to cry, helplessly and unashamedly. Margaret Garrett, bowed silently over a great heap of stockings—convent stories had for some time past been strictly forbidden —shook her head sadly and murmured: "Yes, yes, my child, it has always been thus. . . . Don't you remember how the Princess in the fairy tale had to cry her eyes out in silence for seven long years and scale the Glass Mountain bare-footed and cross the field of thistles before she arrived at her goal?" At these words, Mary's tears suddenly ceased to flow and her eyes flashed a silent challenge.

But there was worse to come. Lady Grace finally decided to write and inform Sir Marmaduke that to all intents and purposes Mary was already as good as a cloistered nun and becoming exceedingly difficult to manage. Possibly a fatherly word or two might be to some purpose.

Sir Marmaduke arrived a week later. He had aged considerably; his hair had gone very grey and he looked careworn and unhappy. The tone he adopted towards his daughter was far more peremptory than she had ever heard him use before. These were not the times, he said,

for a girl to indulge in pious caprices. If, secure in that
haven of peace, she had managed to remain in ignorance
of the misery that was abroad in the land, he could
tell her more than enough about it. The Catholics were
being persecuted even more ruthlessly under James
Stuart than under the late Queen of unhappy memory.
New lists of recusants were continually appearing, "from
which His Majesty had permitted his courtiers to derive
a certain advantage"—in other words, certain noblemen
were being bled white to enable the King's beggarly
Scottish courtiers to wax fat on the proceeds. The
proverb about an Englishman's home being his castle
had become a hollow mockery. There was hardly a
single Catholic family that had not endured the humilia-
tion of domiciliary visits. At any hour of the night,
the emissaries of the law invaded men's homes, hunted
them out of their beds, threatened their women and
children with drawn swords, tore down curtains and
hangings from the walls in search of "idols," tumbled
the beds, demolished walls, often enough even pulled
up the flooring to look for hiding-places, broke locks
and forced open drawers, cupboards and chests. They
wrecked and destroyed what they could like barbarians
as their fancy took them, and carried away with them
letters, silver, books, clothes and money. For some time
past it had become a profitable source of income (and
surely the vilest in God's unhappy world) to denounce
Catholics in order to enrich oneself with the proceeds.
In this way servants bearing a grudge against their
masters, maids discharged by their mistresses, impatient
creditors or vindictive relations were able to pay off old
scores.

Sir Marmaduke stormed up and down the room,
shaking his fists and tearing his hair—never had Mary

seen her placid father thus. As a squire and as a gentleman, what could he do when his tenants came to him
and complained about the foul wrongs they were
obliged to suffer in silence? Whoever was too poor to
pay his fines as recusant had to forfeit two-thirds of his
goods. In the depths of winter, the bailiffs took away
the blankets from the cottagers' beds, sometimes even
the beds themselves, the cloth that in summer had
been spun for the children's winter garments, together
with the poor man's cow or his couple of sheep. The
milk that a poor old man had begged up at the manor
they had poured away on his own hearth and taken
away with them his pannikin and his drinking-mug.
The vestry of the neighbouring Protestant church was
chockful of pots, pans, pewter vessels and tankards from
these and similar sources. And all one could do was to
suffer in silence. He had already forfeited so much of his
own property that he could never hope to compensate
his tenants for all they had lost for the sake of their faith.
Every day four dozen poor folk were fed at his table
and he remitted debts and interest as far as it lay in his
power to do so. But what did it all amount to? Many
preferred to go to prison rather than pay—and everyone
knew what that meant. At York, out of fifty-eight
prisoners, forty had died—of jail fever, so 'twas said.
Or maybe from prison fare. Men feared those jails as
they feared hell.

Small wonder that in many the old fervour had begun
to cool and the old courage to slacken. They were easy
prey for any form of sheer brute force. There were
organized "battues" with themselves as the quarry.
At Hereford there had recently been a big hunt of this
kind over a circuit of some thirty miles—but the hunters
had found nobody save an old woman and a few children,

their quarry having fled over the border to Wales. Only last June on such another occasion, they had come upon eleven villages entirely deserted. The inhabitants had fled to the woods and had lived there for days and nights on end like so many hunted beasts until they had finally plucked up the courage to return to their empty cottages, their looted stables, and ravaged gardens and fields. Could you wonder that many thought God had forsaken them and that maybe the others were right, after all? Could you wonder that apostasy was on the increase?

But what Sir Marmaduke also knew was that up in the north young men were meeting night after night and forging deep-laid schemes. He knew that a great conspiracy was being hatched and that half his kinsfolk were involved: Thomas Percy, his wife's brother-in-law, together with her own brothers, the fighting-cocks John and Christopher, and many others of their kinsfolk. He was fully aware of all this, but he himself would have naught to do with it; he was opposed to violence and was a loyal subject, even of a faithless king. Rebellion was a crime against God and man; there was no blessing on it, and it could only call down a terrible vengeance on many who, as it was, were all too sorely pressed.

But there were other ways, legitimate, pacific ways, and such a one he had in mind. And Mary could help him, no one but Mary.

Rigid and motionless, she sat before him, sensing the entreaty in the trembling hands he laid upon her shoulders. Poor, poor father. Never had she loved him so dearly, so helplessly, so pitifully as now. . . . Whether she remembered Edward Neville, he was asking.

Certainly. Lord Neville had been a frequent guest at Babthorpe, also at neighbouring manors to which she

had been wont to ride over on a visit. His father had
been the paladin of the hapless Queen of Scots and, after
the abortive rising of 1569, had paid for his championship
of a lost cause by the confiscation of his property. In
effect, it had almost cost him his life, but eventually he
had been banished and had left twelve children behind.
. . . Edward Neville had never seceded to the Protestant
faith; in his youth, to be sure, and more or less under
duress, he had attended the services of the Established
Church, but some fifteen years ago he had seen the light,
and, ever since, had been a most loyal and doughty
champion of our cause—are you listening, Mary?—

Yes, she could still recall the long shrewd head, the
peaked brown beard and clear blue eyes, brimming with
kindliness and humour. . . . He was heir presumptive
to the Westmorland title since the Earl had gone into
exile to Flanders. If he succeeded and the whole of that
immense property were thus to pass into Catholic hands,
then the Cause in the north could count on having in
him a staunch adherent—it was impossible to compute
what it might mean, were this to come to pass, for,
candidly speaking, our present monarch was what Her
late Majesty, with all her faults, never was, a weakling,
and mightily impressed by the prestige and wealth of his
nobles.

But—Lord Neville had asserted that he would lay
claim to the Westmorland title only on one condition:
he must be in a position to found a family, in other words,
only if Mary would consent to be his wife. He had met
her at Babthorpe and had realized that in her he had
found the late and last love of his life. Should he fail to
win her, he was firmly resolved to marry no other woman.
Did Mary hear? In this instance it was not the happiness
of some little country squire that was at stake, someone

who would drown his disappointment in a few carouses
and console himself with some other woman—who could
console himself, in fact, with any other woman. . . .
This was the final irrevocable choice of a man in the
prime of life, the finest, noblest flower of chivalry any
maiden's heart could desire. In this marriage was centred
the hope of Catholic England and the dearest, long-
cherished wish of her old father. "You're not going
to be so childish, so foolish"—his voice again rose almost
to a shriek—"so utterly devoid of conscience—by God,
you shan't—As your father I command you, as your
father I forbid you to leave England unless by my
express orders. . . . Do you understand?"

Poor, poor father. Mary still sat there very erect, her
hands tightly clasped in her lap, her face as white as her
own snowy coif.

"Father, I'm sorry, so very sorry, but it's impossible.
I may not obey you."

Poor Lord Neville—he had always been so kind to her,
oh yes, she could not help but notice it, even though she
would never have presumed to interpret the courteous
attentions of a man so much older than herself as anything but courtesy. She respected and esteemed him, nay,
even more, she really liked him and trusted him, warmly
and sincerely, more than any other man she had ever
met—it seemed so hard that she had got to hurt him
now. All she hoped was that she would never have to
meet him again, for that indeed would be truly terrible.

But her father had started again, was shouting, almost
weeping, utterly beside himself.

"What is the good of all your religion if you have
so little love and zeal for God's cause? If all you think
of is yourself? When the sore straits of our brethren in

the faith cannot even prevail upon you to renounce a pretty girlish dream? From whom have you learnt such things? Not from your parents, not from the Babthorpes, nay, not from any of us who have all borne witness to our faith and suffered for it. Must you not blush for very shame recalling the martyrs of our race, Robert Middleton and Edward Thwing, and those others who gave their lives for the Cause? Isn't there any priest who'll bring you, stubborn as you are, to a proper way of thinking?"

And thus it went on and on, the whole evening long.

Completely exhausted, Mary knelt in the chapel whilst Sir Marmaduke sat in council with the other members of the family. So God had sent the cross at last which she had so often read about and for which she so often had prayed. Only it was far, far worse than she had ever dreamt, since it was not she alone who suffered —that would have been sweet indeed—but her father, her loving, beloved father, to whom his child must seem unnatural, disloyal, and, bitterest shame of all, dead to all sense of honour, because she refused to agree to something that to a man of his chivalrous instincts was the only possible choice: to sacrifice herself for their sacred, beloved, suffering Cause. And Lord Neville too. . . .

Fly: Mary uttered the word aloud. She shivered in the chill November air that drifted in, damp and raw, through the open window. She had hurried into the chapel without a wrap, and yet her limbs were burning as though in a fever. Fly! Never to see her father again— another scene like that, she felt, would be more than she could endure. To procure a peasant girl's dress somewhere in the village should not be difficult; the people all knew her and were fond of her. Then she would have to work her way to the coast and find some

E

ship that was due to sail. It was really quite simple.
They were all used to her getting up before the others,
and one morning she'd just go into the garden as usual
and not come back again—no, never again. God would
continue to be her Guide. . . . Then misgivings began
to arise . . . she was not physically strong, not used to
roughing it—Supposing she were to fall sick on the
way, supposing she were to find herself involved in one
of those hunts on Papists. . . .

The Missal lay on the altar. She suddenly recalled
how St. Francis had once sought to learn the will of
God and had received His answer. She opened the book
at random. In the flickering light of the sanctuary lamp,
she could vaguely decipher the great illuminated letters
"Quaerete primum Regnum Dei . . ." Ah, yes—Seek
first the kingdom of God and all the rest will be given
you. Gradually the turmoil died down within her
breast. Father, I too love our holy persecuted Cause,
and every word you uttered seemed to fall on an open
wound. Ever since I can remember, I have dreamt of
shedding my blood some day for our holy faith. . . .
But my hands are tied, I know not why; all I know is
that I am no longer free, not even free to work for the
kingdom of God. . . . That is the hardest thing of all.
But maybe there is a different kind of martyrdom than
that of the body—yes, father, I almost believe there is,
and that such a one has fallen to my lot.

The following days passed in a whirl. Mary had to
pack her things; her father was taking her to London.
He was anxious for her to meet Lord Neville again,
and he also wanted her to consult with Father Holtby,
the aged priest who alone was acquainted with Mary's
convent plans; they would discuss the matter sanely with

the valiant-hearted, saintly priest who could be trusted to approach the matter with sympathy and understanding for both parties. Mary was well content that her projected flight from Babthorpe was thus definitely ruled out. She had a very high opinion of Father Holtby's sagacity; were he to side with her, her father would soon be won over; if not, she must manage to leave London unobserved.

Sir Marmaduke rode on ahead. On the following day she received the news that he had been taken prisoner in Warwickshire with a number of others. He had put up for the night at Aunt Martha's house, and Mark Brittaine, one of her grooms, had managed to escape and bring the news. He did not know what it was all about, but the whole country round was in a fever of excitement. An hour before they had reached Alcester, troops had ridden through from London on their way to Dunchurch, noblemen with their retinues, some eighty men all told, and there were horses, too, belonging to Mr. Catesby. Some said that they were not troops at all, but a large hunting party—or maybe on their way to a wedding. To Sir Everard Digby's . . .

And a few days later, both her aunts were arrested, Dorothy and Margaret, the wives of the Wrights, and laughing Martha, Thomas Percy's wife. . . . A terrible conspiracy had just been discovered in London, thirty-six barrels of gunpowder beneath the Houses of Parliament, a mysterious letter to Lord Monteagle. . . . What they did not know as yet was that on that very day on which the news had arrived, a desperate battle was being fought at Holbeach between the last of the conspirators and the sheriff's men: some gunpowder exploded and a number of the gentlemen were badly hurt. Catesby was burnt to death, the two gallant

Wrights both fell, also their two cousins, the Winters. Thomas Percy, mortally wounded, was conveyed to the Tower where he died a few days later. The whole family was plunged into mourning.

The parting from Babthorpe seemed strangely commonplace and unreal; everyone had other things to think about. Mary donned her travelling cloak and visited once more all the rooms in turn and her beloved chapel. . . . Then it all lay behind her, dim and silent in the falling rain, and another seven years of her life had already become a thing of the past. . . .

At Baldwin's Gardens, in Holborn, she rejoined her father, who had been released, since he had been able to prove that he was innocent of any complicity in the Gunpowder Plot. Little was said between them on the subject, but his every glance and every silence conveyed to her more plainly than ever words could have done: You see how desperate things are. You see to what lengths men can be driven by despair—and not the worst men either.

The following morning before mass, Father Holtby sent her a message saying he would see her in the little white sacristy. Coming straight to the point, he told her that her marriage with Lord Neville was obviously the will of God. He had been her spiritual director and knew of her desire for the religious life—he himself was a religious—but in a case like this there was no choice. The founding of an hereditary Catholic stronghold in the north by the Earl of Westmorland was something of far greater importance than the yearning of a devout maiden for a cloistered life. Her duty lay before her so clearly and simply that, even were she already a novice in some religious order, she could not render God a greater service than by returning to the world and becoming Lord Neville's wife. Obedience was better than sacrifice, and he trusted that she would no longer oppose her father's will but, whilst they were in London, would lose no time in bringing the matter to a satisfactory conclusion.

He dismissed her abruptly with a wave of the hand and at once began to vest himself for mass.

Her face in her hands, Mary knelt motionless in her place, her whole being nerved to one silent agonized entreaty: Lord, do Thou answer for me.

Suddenly she was roused by some unaccustomed sound and discovered to her amazement that mass was already over and the altar cleared. Father Holtby was washing his hands in a corner, and believing herself to be back in the chapel at Babthorpe, she rose from her knees and in her old role of faithful sacristan, tendered him the towel. Then she suddenly realized, with a feeling almost of horror, what it was that had roused her from her meditations. Father Holtby was crying—his grey beard was wet with tears and he was murmuring in broken words interspersed with sobs: "How was it possible, Lord, that I should live to offend Thee?"

He then told Mary what had happened. "God willed it that after the Consecration I upset the chalice—something terrible for a priest—but at the same time I seemed to hear Our Lord say to me: Beware that you spill not yet another chalice of My sacrifice—and I think I know what He meant. Again I wanted to be more far-seeing than Providence itself. Dear child, never again will I oppose your pious resolution, but will try to the best of my ability to convince your good father that it is thus God wills it and not otherwise."

PART II

IT was all over now. The parting from her father, who had suffered it wearily, sadly, but without bitterness. The parting from her beloved big brother. Her mother and the little ones she had not been able to see again. . . . Then came the months spent with relations in London until a ship could be found to run the risk of taking emigrants on board.

It was May; everywhere the young folk in the villages were dancing and singing around the maypole with its garland of green and its fluttering ribbons. . . .

It was Pentecost, and in many a secret chamber hunted priests were celebrating the Holy Sacrifice behind bolted doors and praying to the Spirit of fortitude and strength for their poor, persecuted flock, faithful even unto death.

Mary stood alone on the deck of the *Hind*, which with billowing sails launched out on a glittering blue-grey sea. A regular Pentecost wind came blustering up from the west; slowly the white cliffs of Dover slipped away, the green beloved land of her birth. With an abrupt movement, she turned her back on her native country. "He who hath laid his hand on the plough and looks back is not worthy of me," were the words that were running through her head. But her lips were quivering, quivering so much that she had to clench her teeth until it hurt. The open sea sparkled with a thousand dancing lights. Glass-green in an unending cascade of rippling pearls the waters parted at the bow of the ship. Seagulls shot past, screaming flashes of light; far away in the distance, half hidden in a haze, dawned a blue streak, the coast of Flanders—her promised land. . . . The sun beat fiercely down on her hands, holding the rail in a firm grasp, and on her brown travelling cloak. The whole world was glittering, dancing, and laughing; the wind roared above her so that the strong sails strained and billowed; an exhilarating tang was in the air of high adventure and vast horizons, growing ever stronger, sweeping the ship like the spray of a mighty wave. . . It is Pentecost and the month of May, and I am free!

Suddenly, Mary sank down until she was on her knees, her head buried in her arms, weeping with great sobs as though her heart would break. The violent tension that had hitherto borne her up relaxed and her heart seemed to fail her for utter weariness. She was alone and helpless and sick with fear. She knew not whither she was bound, saw only the sorrowful eyes of her father, and knew that she would never see him again. She wanted to go back to Babthorpe, back home, to England: she wept and wept, until finally she sank on a great coil of rope and fell asleep like a child from sheer exhaustion.

  * * * * *

So this was the new life.

Strange indeed to find oneself on Catholic soil. It was all so very different from what she had imagined. Here they proclaimed from the very house-tops what at home was whispered only in secret chambers. On every house there was some holy image—not just one, but many—over the doors, hewn in stone or carved in wood, grey or many-coloured, between the windows

duty lies clearly before one. Now come, my dear child, your good Mother is waiting!"

*   *   *   *   *

So this was the new life.

A gloomy little parlour in a very old building, almost like a cave hollowed out of a rock, so dark it was and so low. The tiny window lay in a deep slanting shaft in the heavy vaulted ceiling. A single bench of unplaned wood stood beneath it, otherwise the room was quite bare. The opposite wall was partly occupied by a large iron grating, behind which there was another one made of wood, and behind that were heavy wooden shutters. There, too, it smelt of incense, as at the Jesuit College, but it also smelt of other things—herrings and washing, for instance.

The shutter behind the grating opened. In the dim light Mary could just distinguish a dark form with a gleaming patch of white; two pale hands signed her to approach and a quiet impersonal voice informed her that she could take up her quarters at once in the room adjoining the Convent gate that had been occupied by the former doorkeeper. On the morrow she could go on a begging round, and there would be a probationary period of one month before her clothing. Her meals would be handed her at stated hours through the wicket. Was there anything further she required or would like to know? No. Praised be Jesus Christ!

The shutter fell to with a gentle click.

The room adjoining the Convent gate was even smaller, stuffier and gloomier than the one she had just left. The grey walls were damp and stained, great unsightly excrescences formed brown patches edged with white above the miserable pallet-bed in one corner and around a ramshackle old wooden cupboard. It was much as she had always imagined a prison to herself. . . . The bed struck damp and chill and was so dirty that she gave an involuntary shudder of disgust. In the niche by the wicket stood a common earthenware basin containing some cold vegetables and a big slice of very stale bread . . . ah, of course, it was already long past the dinner-hour.

The weeks passed like a dream, a dull, leaden dream, blurred and oppressive. Then one day Mary received the grey habit.

"How devout she is!" whispered the pious matrons and maidens of St. Omer who filled the little church with their voluminous rustling skirts and starched white coifs, unashamedly craning their necks in order to get a better view of the altar. "How white and ethereal she looks—a real lady anyone can see at a glance—how very edifying!—Now she's closed her eyes—you mark my words, she's going to be another of those ecstatic ones like Sister Angeline—What a blessing for the Convent; the last one who used to do the begging was a public scandal . . . you know, of course, why she had to go so suddenly? Well, perhaps some things are best left unsaid. . . . However, up to now, this new one has behaved in a most exemplary way. It's a pleasure giving anything to such a lovely young thing; as I said, it's a blessing for the Convent that they've got her. . . . Now look, mistress, how devoutly she kneels there, for all the world as though she were blind and deaf to all that's going on around her. . . . Oh yes, the Abbess is a shrewd one; even though she's shut away from the outside world she knows what's best for the Convent—

A virtuous and gently bred novice like this one, and one who's come from so far away will bring the Convent into good repute again and the old scandals will soon be forgotten—I suppose it was the Fathers of the English College who arranged it all? Father Keynes, did you say? —Ah, the Reverend Fathers know what they're about. You can trust them to hit the bull's eye every time. It's easy going once you've placed yourself in their hands—Oh, look, Aunt, the new sister's receiving the kiss of peace—really a clothing is most affecting and highly edifying, well worth getting up an hour earlier for. . . . What a sweet young Sister! How blissfully happy she must be to have attained at last the goal of all her dreams. Perhaps she's had to wait for years and years like my cousin Sister Emerentiana—you know the one I mean, of course. . . . Now doesn't she look absolutely transfigured. . . . Ah, a clothing. . . . !"

Mary was back again in the doorkeeper's cell and stood there in her heavy grey habit, pale as death, with her hands tightly clasped. Well, that too was over now. And yet that very morning, in those brief wild moments when her soul had awakened as though from a swoon, her first thought had been: Rather death, a thousand times rather death—oh, far rather the cart rolling on its way to Tyburn as once I saw it in a dream!

But again she had heard that other voice that would not be gainsaid: Qui vos audit, audit me. . . .

They must know better, those men and women in religion, the Father and the nuns who had grown from childhood to maturity in that holy land into which she had drifted like a bird that had lost its way.

A sublime and holy state . . . those who embrace it must be perfect indeed. . . .

Who had said that . . . said it so often that the words
had left her no peace and she had had to cross the sea
to find the Paradise that the homeland had lost?

Oh Margaret Garrett, was that all you saw—the tall
lilies in the cloisters, the crimson roses twining round
the fountain cross, the chanting choir—and knew you
naught of the silly envious tittle-tattle that finds its way
even past the wicket, naught of the spiritual pride and
aloofness keeping the newcomer ever at a distance,
naught of the unkind words that the few French lay-
sisters pass on to me at the gate till I can listen to them
no longer? Is it true that the Mother Abbess told the
novice-mistress that begging was hardly the kind of thing
I ought to be doing but that they had to think of the
Convent's interests and that my face happened to be the
right kind of talisman to make even the close-fisted give?
Is it true that quite recently in the parlour when certain
ladies, residents of the town, who had called to discuss
spiritual things with her, expressed surprise about the
new Sister chosen for the begging rounds and remonstrated
with her for allowing so young and, as they pleased to
put it, so fair a girl to be out in the streets all day alone
(adding that the burdens I had to carry were far beyond
my strength and that anyone could see that I was not
trained to such hard work), did she really tell them that
it had been *my* dearest wish, that in a very excess of
humility I had begged to be allowed to help the cloistered
Sisters thus and that she herself had not dared to oppose
the promptings of the Holy Ghost? Sister Jacqueline
heard her, and she understands French. The ladies had
gone away most edified. . . . Lies, lies . . . but whose
lies? Sister Jacqueline doesn't tell lies, she's a fishing girl
from these parts, sturdy, simple, somewhat uncouth, but
she's good. . . . She believed every word of it and told

me the whole story in wide-eyed amazement. She even wanted to know whether I had had my instructions directly from the lips of an angel. . . .

Was it true that this was not the first time either that the Abbess had told such a tale? That she had said: "As, of course, everybody knows," that she had said: "Only ask Father Keynes; he is her spiritual director and he, too, is frankly amazed at her humility, but the desire of a soul to attain perfection will not be gainsaid." Was it all true?

In her despair, she sought out the novice-mistress, who, like herself, was from England, and who was the only one with whom she could converse in her own language. Her heart ached almost beyond endurance with a tremendous longing for home, and she could have fallen on the neck of the tall gaunt woman when she heard the first familiar words of her own mother-tongue. But Mother Stephana Googe proved cold and censorious, read her a sharp homily on frowardness, distrust, and stiff-necked worldly pride that presumed to sit in judgment on its superiors, and concluded by giving her a penance.

Ah, it was better to think of nothing, nothing at all—thinking hurt so. It was better to get down to work, work that dinned, harassed, and tired you to death; that helped. . . .

So this was the religious life.

At Babthorpe, I thought it meant just kneeling at the feet of the Most High, and I trained and prepared myself to that end. . . . Oh, the morning stillness, when book in hand, I walked beneath the ancient trees, across the dewy grass that spread unheeded over the paths through the park, and dreamt of the Cistercian cloisters at Eshwold. . . . Oh, evening peace in the stillness of the chapel,

F

when every candlestick glittered in the jewelled light filtering in through the windows, when the sanctuary lamp swung gently to and fro and my cousins knelt in their pews like tall comely statues on dead knights' tombs. . . . Oh the holy enchantment of those nights full of the mystery of His nearness, when, shoes in hand, I crept down the staircase to hold my vigil in that beloved intimate darkness. . . . That was a spiritual life in very truth; in those days there always seemed to be time for a quiet breathing-space, for prayer and recollection.

Now all day long, she trudged through streets and alleys, setting out at dawn with the empty baskets. Those morning hours were still quiet, so quiet that you could almost think of Divine things, had there not been the endless sums you had to work out in your head. . . . Then the road led out of the town through the outlying villages which, with their floating gardens, straggled along the endless straight canals that watered a country as flat as the palm of your hand. The roads were very muddy and the people were busily bent on their work and did not like being disturbed; but they gave all the same, for they had enough and to spare, and they were not stingy. The baskets soon filled up with cabbages, turnips, carrots and beets, with lentils and peas and beans, and sometimes they would throw in a great loaf or two of bread or an enormous flaring bunch of flowers for the chapel. It was very kind of them, of course, but dragging everything home when you were already tired, dead-tired—still tired from your pallet-bed on which it was barely possible to stretch yourself out full-length (her predecessor, Mary surmised, must have been very short indeed)—well, it was hard indeed, for it meant hurrying back as fast as you could, panting for breath and bathed in perspiration, in order to be home before noon. The baskets were handed over at the gate, and she would then hurriedly (often standing) swallow her little basin of food at the wicket. After that, it began all over again, and she would set out on the second round with an aching back and soaking wet shoes, and with feet getting ever more sore and inflamed.

But that was not the worst by any means, no, not even that badly ulcerated knee of hers, the result of a fall on the slippery margin of the canal, which kept her awake the greater part of the night—(sometimes she ruefully smiled to herself, remembering that once upon a time she had thought the wearing of a wire girdle to be a penance!) Worst of all were the people. . . . They didn't mean it, of course, but when you'd lived all your life in country manors surrounded by great gardens amongst courtly gentlemen and noble ladies of genuine piety, you couldn't help finding the people you met in the streets and public places very rough and crude . . . but that, again, only went to show how proud and worldly-minded you still were at heart.

At first, too, she could not understand the language, though that didn't matter so very much; everything was still so strange and new, with a lingering touch of enchantment. It made her think of that time at home when some of her young kinsmen had staged a merry little comedy; she was quite small then and sat so far back in the room that she could see only the strange costumes and extravagant gestures, but was unable to catch a single word. But now it was different; she was beginning to understand, and it was awful. When she had to wait outside an open door or by a garden-fence, she could not help hearing everything the women were discussing, all the gossip and scandals of the little town, and her eyes were opened to a horrified realization of what the world was really like. . . . At home her father had sent every maid packing who was caught uttering a coarse word before the children—and those mysterious whispered confabulations between Aunt Martha and her maid Meg—oh, how silly they all seemed compared with what she was now compelled to listen to day after day blared forth at the top of people's voices to the accompaniment of shrieks of laughter, with never a thought for the habit she wore. Men loafing outside the taverns tried to catch hold of her as she passed and shouted things after her that made her blood boil within her, and she flared at them in white-hot indignation so that, cursing, they turned on their heel and went their ways. And then, after it was all over, she had nearly swooned for fear and mortal shame. She wept burning suffocating tears over her outraged dignity and because she durst not seek retaliation—and because she was what she was and all her nature panted to be avenged—and because of the utter misery of this mortal life of ours. And it was but a poor consolation, or rather rubbing salt and ashes in her wounds, when the old French lay Sister who relieved her of her baskets at the gate said with a shrug: "Don't take it so much to heart, little one—the last Sister who went your round, you see, was such a one that they still think you're likely to be amused by that sort of thing."

A sublime and holy state. . . . Those who embrace it must be perfect. . . . Ah, would I had never heard those words!

Mother Mary Stephana, the novice mistress, told her to seek consolation in prayer and to discuss her temptations with her spiritual director. . . . But how was she to pray in that utter darkness and apathy, in which the exhausted aching body weighed down the soul like a leaden burden, crushing it back to earth as soon as it tried to wing its flight to heaven?

Never a moment had she to herself, not even on her endless rounds, for her face had proved so powerful a talisman in loosening tight-fisted hands, as the Abbess called them, that she received more than she was able to carry and now had to take Sister Jacqueline along with her, who dinned her with her unceasing chatter.

At night, she sank on her pallet half-dead with exhaustion, so dog-tired that not even the gnawing pain in her ulcerated knee could keep her awake. Prayer! How poor she had become, how exceeding poor! No, never before had she realized that a human being could be so utterly destitute as not even to find the time to pray, time for a brief space of quiet breathing for his harassed soul.

And that was not true either, that solemn assurance that Father Keynes had dangled like a bait before her: that there was but *one* holy rule for choir and lay sisters alike. No longer had she any part in the Divine Office of the Church that had been the very pulse of her spiritual life ever since she had been able to read. Her big Psalter had been stowed away in a corner of the ramshackle cupboard near the door, and there it remained, mildewed and mouldering. She was shut out from that wondrous ever-recurring round of the Church's holy seasons, from feasts and fasts, from the solemn procession in the company of holy martyrs and virgins, bishops and confessors, abbots and apostles, doctors and holy women. The rule she had received was that of the Third Order, and her Office consisted of an endless succession of Our Fathers that Sister Jacqueline blared forth to the world at large in a stentorian singsong as they went their rounds, striding along bravely in time to their rhythm.

To discuss matters with her spiritual director was frankly impossible. Not merely because talking about oneself had always been so difficult and embarrassing —ah, here she had learnt what begging meant, and not only for bread and meat—but it was so depressing and humiliating when after weeks of self-torment, you had nerved yourself to make the effort, and, trembling and hesitant, had bared your poor suffering soul before the physician, only to realize that the good Father Guardian had not understood a single word of it all—yes, her French, she feared, was still very halting. And though Father Keynes would, of course, have understood their common tongue, she avoided him on his frequent visits to the Convent with gentle obstinacy. Had he not said before her clothing: "If an angel from heaven were to come and order you to leave this convent, do not believe him; rather laugh him to scorn as a delusion sent by the devil—God hath called you as surely to this state as St. Paul's hour before Damascus was also from God."

And now, thought Mary with a bitter little smile that brought a rush of tears to her eyes, now it is he who has transformed himself into that same angel from heaven. . . . Having finally made up my mind to live and die where I am, without murmur or complaint, having implored Our Lord to grant me His peace—and, perhaps, just a little joy—the Father now must come and say: "It cannot possibly be God's will that you remain here!"

No, no, I don't want to hear another word on the subject. It's best to have converse with God alone. Even if He gives you no answer—or even if you're so tired that you don't hear His voice—at least He doesn't say things that confuse you. Under obedience I came here, and only under obedience will I go.

You got used to so much. You learnt, for instance, to carry your baskets in such a way that they no longer galled your shoulders; your feet accustomed themselves in time to wooden shoes, your body to the heavy loads, your digestion to *warremus* and the bitter small beer of the country, even to the lamp-oil in which the pease were cooked during Lent.

People, too, were really good at heart, courageous and generous. Mary often felt ashamed that the fine lady in her had been so terribly shocked at the rough, blunt ways that these members of God's great family just happened to have been born with. God's grace, after all, was not set apart for delicate breeding, soft voices and a dignified bearing. She had even learnt to face the fact that priests were not invariably what she had been wont to imagine them in England, all holy confessors and a higher order of beings, enshrouded in an atmosphere of mystery and adventure, ever surrounded with the crimson aureole of martyrdom—but that there were also such as stood with their feet firmly—sometimes a little too firmly—planted on this earth of ours, who loved a good table, and a good cellar even more; men with faces like full moons and fine costly raiment, men who were connoisseurs of wine and connoisseurs of horseflesh, fine gentlemen who rode a-hunting and returned o' nights escorted by a crowd of pages with torches and a blare of minstrelsy from the mansions of the rich; and others, men of the people, who looked as though they might be up to any of the tricks that were retailed with such infinite gusto about that merry rascal Tyl Uilenspiegel.

The sun rose every morning above the trailing veils

of silvery mist that hung over the floating gardens as once over Babthorpe Park. Larks without number carolled high in the moist blue air; the squat bastions, pillars and many towers, both round and square, of the city walls, with their soft greys and yellows, their red brickwork and thick cloak of ivy, gleamed as though freshly washed in the clear early-morning light over the misty blue-green plain. The wet roofs of innumerable church-towers soared like lambent streaks of silver against the soft fleecy whiteness of the sky; invisible bells unceasingly sang out their benediction on the land and men in the fields and gardens doffed their caps and made the sign of the cross.

Faith here, thought Mary, was like one's good daily bread; a bit stale, and in some cases, maybe, a trifle mouldy, but, in spite of everything, daily bread, the good, firm, brown earth beneath· one's feet, barely heeded, passed over in silence, but from which everything grows in rich, life-giving abundance, all the good sober things of our daily life. . . . To us, the Faith is something quite different—something altogether out-of-the-ordinary, enchanted, and thrilling, an eternal fairy story . . . intoxicating, with a strange exhilarating tang . . . an exotic mysterious bloom from another world, anxiously tended and fostered within secret walls, watered with red blood, guarded with gleaming swords. . . . It is the Faerie Queen whom knights errant serve . . . not, as here, the good mother of a large family, doling out to her children their slices of daily bread. . . . The other kind—our kind—in its way, is attractive too; but this here is healthier, simpler . . . more real. We ought to be able to grow up in a country like this, to be able to send for our children and have them reared over here in a land where priests don't appear and disappear like

a genie that lives in a bottle, where the church is our
Father's house, in which you are free to come and go
just as you please . . . where there's no call to feel oneself
rather interesting and uncommon, or like somebody out
of a ballad, just because one says one's rosary.

O England, my England! when will come the time
when you will be once more a smiling garden of God,
where the hands of His workers may sow the good seed
openly before the eyes of all men, tend His blossoming
plants, and reap His golden harvest? She stretched out
her arms to face the wind that blew lustily with a sharp
tang of salt in its breath from the west, from the seas
that bounded her own native-land.

"Are you feeling homesick, Sister?" Jacqueline asked
her gently—she knew that feeling, even though the
home she had left behind her was not quite so far away
and but a little fishing-hut on a dreary sand-flat.

"Homesick?" said Mary. "No, I think it's something
more than that. I feel as though my country is trying
to send me some message—just as though with myriad
fingers it were tapping at my heart—you know, like
captives sending messages to one another in prison—
only as yet I don't seem to understand what the message
is."

*   *   *   *   *

It was March the twelfth, the Feast of St. Gregory—
"My patron," Mary explained to the faithful Jacqueline,
who listened open-mouthed to her every word. "*Our*
patron, I should say. He sent the first missionaries to
England, you know."

And whilst the two young Sisters picked out and sorted
the contents of their sacks and baskets in the gloomy cell

beside the Convent gate, Mary told the Fleming the old familiar story: How in the slave market of Rome, amongst captive Ethiopians, Syrians, lithe brown Egyptians and other dusky folk, Pope Gregory had singled out the milk-white, flaxen-haired Angles, and, struck by their beauty and the angelic association conjured up by their name, had decided then and there that they too should be saved: how the monk Augustine sailed for the islands with forty brethren: how whilst King Ella was quaffing his mead amongst his warriors in his great hall, the winter wind blew a sparrow that had lost its way in through the open door and out again into the dark night, and how an old warrior spoke: Like the flight of that bird is the life of man, O King— none knoweth whence he came nor whither he goes. If these men can tell us the answer, then, methinks, they should be permitted to speak. . . .

Holy Father, St. Gregory, when are you going to send another emissary to my people?

"This afternoon we shan't have to do the second round," Sister Jacqueline was saying. "It's Visitation Day. The Father General is here. You'll be sure to see him, Sister, for he always asks to see the English nuns. He's a terribly learned gentleman and rules over all the convents in Flanders and North Germany, in Ireland and Lorraine—though he himself is a Spaniard and the confessor of the Regent in Brussels."

That same afternoon Mary found herself in due course in the presence of the great man, whose eyes surveyed her from beneath dark heavy lids and who asked her a few questions in fairly good English.

Yes, she was quite well, she said, but then, she just happened to be young and strong. She did not think

that her countrywomen found it easy to adapt themselves
to the life of Flemish convents, even though so many of
them came over to enter religion there.

The General arched his brows inquiringly. They
were, Mary explained, encouraged by a friendly nod,
mostly women of gentle birth who had never done any
hard work in their lives, and yet from the first day they
were expected to launder heavy woollen garments, to
wash in lye, to repair the broken flagstones in the cloisters
and to handle the mighty looms, a task better fitted for
men or for the sturdy daughters of Dutch farmers.
It was not pride that urged her to tell him these things;
the majority shouldered the burden with a right good
will and for the love of God—but, for all that, it didn't
seem quite right. The soul sickened, when the body
weighed it down with suffering and weariness that
were beyond its strength. After all, one entered a convent with the idea of serving God with prayer and
meditation, but this life was nothing but dull, dogged
endurance, as it is written in the words of the Psalmist:
"I am become as a beast before thee, O God."

"Hm," mused the Visitor, stroking his long black
beard, then asked her what she thought he could do
in the matter.

He was the General Commissioner and free to act as
he thought fit, said Mary simply and without a trace of
embarrassment. As the two local Poor Clare communities consisted in either case of both Flemish and
English Sisters, he could separate the nuns according
to their mother-tongue and thus form two uniform
communities, each with a house of its own and under
the direction of priests of their own nationality. The
latter arrangement, she added with a wry little smile,
recalling her own experiences in the past, would also

be more conducive to the spiritual advancement of each community.

"Hm," said the Father Guardian once more, still stroking his beard. "Your little suggestion unfortunately is not practicable, as the two Convents at St. Omer do not observe the self-same rule. But you certainly appear to have given a considerable amount of thought to these matters."

"Yes," said Mary. "I'm an Englishwoman, you see, and what we have to endure for the sake of our faith makes for solidarity. So even in a convent one seems to go on worrying and making plans."

"Hm," was again the Vicar General's only comment, though there was a glint of interest in his heavy eyes. And she was a lay-sister there? And what was her work? Begging? Gold seemed to be fairly plentiful in the streets of St. Omer that they could afford to use it for paving-stones. Shaking his head, he laughed silently to himself, and Mary began to feel somewhat uneasy. Then quite suddenly he laid his hand on her head— tall as she was, this Spaniard was even taller—and now his eyes were very wide awake and very, very kind, as he said in his queer foreign English: "You have not yet been professed and are still perfectly free. Leave this convent and do so as soon as possible, do you understand? This is something that shrieks to heaven—who is the fool responsible for such a state of affairs? Do you choose some other way of serving His Divine Majesty, and if I can assist you in any wise, I will do so right willingly."

After that there was a brief and stormy conference between the Father Guardian, the Abbess, the Novice-Mistress and Father Keynes, the latter solemnly protesting that he had long said the same thing and that he would know no peace until this unfortunate matter—already the talk of the town—was satisfactorily settled.

Sister Jacqueline, who by some mysterious process always got wind of everything, made off with the news in hot haste for the gate, only to creep back feeling very small indeed.

In her dark little cell Mary was on her knees, her pale face illumined with a light that dimmed the feeble glimmer of the guttering tallow candle, and with the tears streaming unheeded down her cheeks and hands upraised she sang to herself over and over again:

"Anima nostra sicut passer erepta est de laqueo venatium, laqueus contritus est, et nos liberati sumus."[1]

A fortnight later, the General Visitor of the Franciscans, who had returned to the court of Brussels, emerged after his thanksgiving from the black and gold sacristy to find a young girl in a brown travelling cloak and a steeple-crowned hat awaiting him at the door.

"Do you remember?" Mary reminded him. "I've come to Brussels to discuss the foundation of an English convent of the Poor Clares with the Regent. I have English letters of recommendation for her from my cousin Lady Mary Percy of the Benedictine Convent here, but if I may make so bold as to remind you of a certain promise. . . ."

The interview took place in the Infanta's private cabinet. Tall and stout, with a comfortable double-chin emerging from innumerable rows of pearls, Isabella did not impress Mary as too alarmingly regal. She had already heard much about her untiring generosity towards

[1] Our soul hath been delivered: as a sparrow out of the snare of the fowlers.
The snare is broken and we are delivered.

all religious institutions and of her special interest in Catholic émigrées. Archduke Albert with his thin blond beard and his short-sighted blue eyes reminded her very much of Sir Ralph Babthorpe, and, as one of his sisters was a Poor Clare in Madrid, Mary felt, if only on that account, that he would be favourably disposed towards her scheme.

In a clear matter-of-fact voice, but with eyes sparkling with enthusiasm, she outlined her plans to the royal couple and the Franciscan General, who sat there, again with half-closed lids and still stroking his beard. There was a crying need for a convent for Englishwomen of gentle birth who came to the Continent with a desire to enter religion. St. Clare's Rule was to be observed in its primitive simplicity, the food, however, and the work done to make the institute self-supporting, to be adapted to conform with the English mode of life. His Grace, Bishop Blaise of St. Omer, himself a son of St. Francis, the Lord Abbot of St. Bertin and the Father Rector of the English College had already given their approval to the scheme.

"And the Holy Father in Rome, too, I suppose?" inquired Father Andrew Soto grimly.

"No," said Mary in all innocence. That wasn't necessary. The Lord Bishop of Ypres in whose diocese the house was situated had also been consulted.

"House? What house?"

Why, the house for the new foundation; she would certainly never have dreamt of troubling Their Highnesses, had not things been at least as far advanced as that. It was a fine big house in the village of Ecchelstbeker, just outside Gravelines, and it had often struck her when she was on her begging rounds as admirably suited for the purpose. The English Fathers had nego-

tiated the purchase with Count de Guernouval, the
Governor of Gravelines, and the ten thousand gulden
had already been deposited in the presence of witnesses.

"And who provided the money?" asked the Regent.

"Why, I did," said Mary in surprise. "My dowry
was returned to me when I left the convent—so, of course,
I did not like to ask other people to finance my scheme."

"How much have you left over for yourself?" asked
the Regent again. The Archduchess was staring at her
in speechless amazement.

"Oh, I'm not anxious on that score," Mary replied
laughing. "As soon as I have your gracious permission,
I intend to enter the convent myself."

*   *   *   *   *

Things, however, did not move quite so smoothly
as she had anticipated. Weeks were wasted in endless
negotiations with the court of Brabant, weeks of ceremoni-
ous calls, of long patient waiting in the antechambers of
princes and prelates until all those set in authority had
had their say, until all formalities had been complied
with and all susceptibilities taken into due account.
The pages and ladies-in-waiting who whispered and
chattered on every staircase and in every corner in French,
Flemish, German and Spanish, soon began to recognize
and salute with a kind of respectful curiosity the tall,
slender girl in the béguine-like grey dress as she passed
in and out of the cabinets of the great. Long hours
were spent with the Archduke's secretary, dictating,
reckoning, signing documents, until the estate had
changed hands, another security had been deposited with
the authorities, another house been taken at St. Omer to
shelter the community pending completion of their

new convent, and until the Bishop's permission had been secured for every individual Sister who was being taken over from other religious houses. Was this, she wondered, the new work for the kingdom of God—documents and yet more documents, a welter of ink, red tape, couriers' fees and legal clauses. I suppose, though, it must be, thought Mary resignedly; there were always fresh surprises in store for you when you were trying to do the will of God.

Then finally, that, too, was over. In a quiet alley, looking very new and still smelling of raw timber and fresh paint, stood the new Convent of the Poor Clares; the chapel was consecrated at last and in the light-grey corridors and rooms the young English community lived and went about their appointed tasks.

And then the clothing was over—Mary's second clothing, as different from the first as the quiet solemnity of that radiant June morning, sweet with the fragrance of roses and lilies, was different from the leaden days of mud and fog on the roads near Gravelines. Like a dream, the last eighteen months gradually slipped away; unsubstantial and unreal as any dream, the memory of the court of Brussels faded in its turn. . . . This, at last, was the haven, the ultimate goal—home. This was the religious life for which the heart of the seventeen-year-old girl, sitting at the feet of Margaret Garrett, had craved. It was like living again those blissful years of her youth at Babthorpe, only infinitely sweeter, more full of meaning, for all that had been a child's play and this, this was reality.

The austere rule of St. Clare was observed in its primitive simplicity. Meat was never seen on their table, not even for the sick. One single meal a day sufficed; only on the high feast of Christmas were they permitted a second repast. Instead of linen, the sisters wore a material of coarse texture next the skin, slept on straw and rose at midnight to sing the Divine Office. Silence reigned in the house of Gravelines practically the whole day. It was all just as it should be. It was all as the Saints had taught. The world was remote, submerged. It was but rarely that anyone knocked at their door. Somewhere, very far off, human life rushed on like a mighty river. She was living again on that holy island that no other foot might tread. What matter that the whole year long you were so hungry that you could hardly sleep. The pangs of mortifications were to God like the fragrance of a burnt offering. The impetuous heart had grown very still. Now all was well. All was as it should be.

It was May the second, the feast of the holy Bishop and Confessor Athanasius. They had heard the Gospel from the tenth chapter of St. Matthew in which you could almost hear the rolling of distant thunders presaging danger and distress, flight, persecution and violent death. In the old days of their English homeland it had all seemed very close and real; now they heard it intoned from the altar, and it was just as though they heard the meaningless rumbling of a distant storm that had passed over. On plain deal benches in the cloisters, the Sisters sat at their morning task of plaiting St. Francis girdles for the use of religious, Mary softly reciting to herself the while the Litany of Loreto in the intention that the future wearer of the girdle she was making might be preserved from mortal sin.

Then, without any warning, it happened: something inexplicable, never experienced before. In a tremendous silent impact her soul was hurled as it were to the ground,

G

and she found herself enveloped in a blinding light; relentlessly the Divine Will bore down on her with the inexorable swoop of an eagle. For an agonized half-hour, she seemed to hang over an abyss, ravaged and torn by the silent, invisible, blinding light of ecstasy.

In complete silence, the Sisters placidly went on with their work; their eyes, piously lowered, saw nothing, neither the icy deathly pallor of the youngest novice nor how pitifully her work shook in her convulsively twitching hands. In that complete stillness, the song of the finches rose loud and clear from the white cherry tree-tops in the convent garden. A day like any other day. . . .

The sound of the midday bell chimed clearly through the house; the long line of nuns with lowered veils hurried into the little grey chapel and the antiphon rose from the choir. It was all just as usual. Nobody was aware that anything extraordinary had happened. Nobody knew that before their very eyes God's lightning had struck that peaceful house that a woman had builded to shelter her for a life-time. Nobody knew that Mary now moved and took her place amongst them like a fugitive who seats himself for a night at the hospitable board of a stranger, like an outcast who has no abiding city.

Once more she must go her way. That alone she knew, clearly and inexorably, when she came to herself after that blinding shock of illumination. The house she had built was no longer her home. She had been torn by the roots from that consecrated, beloved soil, in which she had thought to blossom and bear fruit until her happy end. Every object, place, and person had suddenly become touched with the agonizing tenderness of a last farewell, transfiguring them with that familiar shimmering radiance that constantly brought the tears in a gush to her eyes. She felt she wanted to cling fast to them all, knowing full well that everything would gently yet surely slip away beneath her hands. She no longer belonged. She belonged nowhere. Was there really any such thing—a person who belonged nowhere? No, there was no road that she could see before her; she was just pitilessly turned adrift at the threshold— and beyond that threshold the ground suddenly broke off at her very feet.

Mother Mary Stephana, erstwhile exacting yet beloved, novice-mistress of St. Omer and now their even more exacting Abbess, loved and revered by Mary with a wistful, worshipping devotion, sent her packing in high displeasure when she fell at her feet, confessing what had befallen her. The times were past when young religious had visions. Such things were obviously a snare of the devil, sent as a punishment for secret pride and to be overcome only by prayer, fasting and penance. Did she really imagine, just because she had been used as an instrument of Providence for the foundation of their house, that it would always be thus and that wherever she went she would continue to be an exception to the general rule? Whenever she felt herself a prey to such fancies, she was to leave whatever work she was doing and apply the discipline as often as was necessary: that was the best way of dealing with such maggots.

Silently Mary kissed the ground and retired. Her spiritual director expressed himself in much the same terms when Mary asked his advice. She would do better to be more punctilious in her observance of their holy rule instead of hankering to go her own foolish ways. She ought to be glad at last to have found a home and a definite aim in life, glad at last to be permitted to serve the Lord in so perfect a way, instead of chasing will-o'-the-wisps and wantonly playing fast and loose with her holy vocation.

Thanks to all her penitential exercises, Mary soon began to go about looking like a living corpse. It was no good. The inner voice pursued her day and night. Willingly she would have performed ten times more penances could she but have found peace. Ah, how little they knew her, those censorious superiors of hers, who deemed her fickle and unstable, ever yearning for something new. With every fibre of her being, she clung desperately to the beloved home that was fast slipping away. How easy in comparison had been the parting from her native-country. Was it possible that the firm conviction that had hitherto supported her and helped her for seven long years to persevere along her self-appointed path had been but a snare of the devil? A vain delusion that inner light, the yearning, the clear call to the religious life? Imagination, everything upon which she had built the entire fabric of her life, for the sake of which she had left her native-country to sail across the sea? Had she no part amongst those chosen ones privileged to follow Our Lord along the path of perfection? Or—like a fever this fear tormented her—had the vocation for the cloistered life been hers (for she found it impossible to doubt the whole of her life hitherto), and had she lost it? And, if so, wherein had she been to blame? Was it a punishment that she was to be cast once more on a world that she had renounced for ever?

There was nobody to whom she could turn for help. Stern and sorrowful looks from the Superior. The Sisters were asked to pray for her, and they cast furtive, pitying, questioning, frightened glances in her direction.

Somehow, the strange story had broken the bounds

of the enclosure. The tongues of the pious gossips of the town were already wagging about the crazy foreigner whose pride had gone to her head, for whom the holy rule of St. Clare wasn't quite good enough, and who assuredly one day would come to a bad end. After all, it was only what was to be expected. A girl who took her vocation seriously did not gad about visiting the courts of princes, and alone into the bargain. There was something decidedly queer about that Brussels trip, when you came to think of it.

Then, one day, Father Lee told her with an ungracious shrug of his shoulders: "You can save your soul whether you stay or go."

It was not much, but it was enough.

The Abbess, too, abandoned her attitude of open hostility for a pained silence. On Palm Sunday, a grey, ice-cold day of March, Mary left the choir quietly after Prime. In the little room by the gate, she doffed the livery of St. Clare, rope, girdle and habit, veil and bandeau, kissing every article reverently on her knees.

Horror-struck, the little Sister at the gate gazed after her as she passed through, and the tears streamed down her face: "That you could be faithless to Our Lord!" she murmured, as in her old grey travelling dress, her shorn hair hidden beneath a coif, Mary moved along the narrow street in the direction of the market-place.

PART III

IT seemed strange to be hiring a room and discussing with the woman of the house her terms for board and lodging—strange to have to reckon with money. Strange to find herself once more amongst people who talked all day long. The children playing in the streets called after her: "Runaway nun! False prophetess!" Kind friends paid calls savouring more of curiosity than sympathy, gave her a lot of good advice, sighed their regrets, lent her biographies of St. Teresa and other saints likely to help her to mend her ways, and, taking all in all, enjoyed themselves immensely. As time went on, even this sensation began to pall, especially as Mary with gentle obstinacy parried every question, showed herself deaf to every prompting, indulged in no confidences, and appealed to no one for help or consolation. Her visitors retired feeling distinctly piqued; of course, if certain people failed to appreciate help when it was offered them, they were beyond all aid. She had made her bed, and must lie on it.

At the Wards' town house, where Sir Marmaduke and the entire family had been in residence for some time past, very little comment was made when Mary made her appearance, following on a brief message announcing her arrival. They left her in peace and she was deeply grateful that everyone behaved as though it were the most natural thing in the world that she should have suddenly materialized in their midst and be looking after her younger sisters and helping her mother. Sir Marmaduke informed her drily that since her absence, Lord Neville

87

had entered the Jesuit College at St. Omer—no, she
herself had heard nothing of it. The status of Catholics
in England had not undergone any material change;
living in London was, if anything, less precarious. Her
two sisters, Elizabeth and Barbara, as she was aware,
were now of a marriageable age. The proximity of
the court was less dangerous than living in the country.
Mary quietly adapted herself to her new mode of life.

"So you've returned to the world?" her kinsfolk and
acquaintances would say, discreetly curious. "A convent,
after all, is no place for a young woman of good birth,
is it? Perhaps you found the life too austere? One
certainly does occasionally hear some very strange
things. . . ."

The older ladies shook their heads with indulgent
smiles. Ah yes, that was just like turbulent youth! The
loftiest peak had to be taken by storm, the wildest things
attempted. . . . Later on one grew more reasonable in
one's ambitions, more content with the beaten track.
This disappointment, no doubt, would be a good lesson
to her, and by now, presumably, she would have profited
by it. In other days, she had abstained from every form
of amusement as though our harmless little pleasures
were, heaven only knew, how sinful and worldly and
altogether beneath her notice. Nowadays she no longer
seemed to be taking such a jaundiced view of things. She
was to be seen at every fashionable function, even at
dances, garden parties and the play, also in the gondolas
and barges that, garlanded and brave with armorial
bearings, drifted down the Thames whilst the minstrels
on board discoursed sweet music. . . . Possibly after her
long and bitter experience of convent life, she hungered a
little after the once despised pleasures of the world. . . .
After all, she was still young . . . even though no longer

of the youngest . . . and she was really lovely, very lovely. . . . Who could tell? . . .

Thus the ladies discussed her, watching her surreptitiously with meaning little smiles from behind their big fans. Mary let them whisper. What a blessing that they were so blind, so unsuspecting, so entirely absorbed and bound up in their own narrow little circle that they had not as much as the slightest inkling of what was going forward.

Mary was now conscious of a new urge, the instinct of the hunter. And her hunting-ground was the city of London, in its entire length and breadth—first and foremost, the court and the high places. How well she had learnt to use her eyes in those long, dolorous months at St. Omer; how responsive and obedient she had become to God's will during those long blissful months of her novitiate.

The eyes that in the devout years of her girlhood had been centred alone on interior things, so that the outside world had slipped by in a kind of dreamy twilight, had suddenly become as keen and alert as those of a royal falcon. She saw around her shifty, wavering eyes and others, dim and tired, above starched ruffs and beneath jauntily nodding plumes. She knew the meaning of the bitter tiny lines around painted lips, that had grown thin and hard with concealed anguish, or loose and irresolute with weakness and self-indulgence. She saw right through their brave attire into the hearts of men, and they were all the same, all poor, hungry, unhappy, hopeful, despairing. She saw all the secret longing and the torturing ache of home-sickness gnawing at the hearts of those who had abandoned the faith for the sake of honour and earthly possessions. She knew how weary, despairing and embittered were the hearts of those who outwardly were still loyal and steadfast to their ancient allegiance. She sensed how heavily their ignorance oppressed them, mockingly assailed with questions they were unable to answer; she knew the toils that were laid for them and how helpless and perplexed they were, hemmed in by enemies on all sides and unattainable for the few priests who travelled about in every sort of disguise, but the very nature of whose work demanded the utmost circumspection. Were all these souls to be lost for God? Why should she repel them by appearing before them in an unfamiliar garb? Why should she avoid those paths where alone they were to be found?

You could talk about God also in the park or over a game, in the alcove of a ball-room, during the interval of a concert, beneath the crimson canopy of a Thames barge—then, softly and adroitly, with unerring aim, fire the crucial question like an arrow sure of its mark.

Sedately pacing the garden pleasances during the intervals of a dance, you could explain the catechism to your partner, inform him in a whisper where the Holy Sacrifice was to be celebrated on the morrow; in a confidential chat behind your fan unravel his perplexities of heart and mind, discourse on the sufferings of confessors in prison, reveal to him in strict confidence when the next ship was due to sail for St. Omer.

Taking your ease on costly rugs spread on the lawn and surrounded by a glittering bevy of fair ladies, you could read to them from the Fathers to the strains of sweet minstrelsy from behind the clipt yew hedges, instruct converts, deal lovingly and understandingly with cases of conscience, or solicit alms for the poor and the persecuted brethren in the faith.

On a morning ride you could prepare some younger

friend for confession or dilate on the excellence of the hidden life of Christ and on the shining virtues of the great religious orders, until, the latent spark kindled to a divine flame, she pledged herself to choose the steep ascent of Mount Carmel or to become one of the family of St. Benedict. Oh, so much could be done of which you had never dreamt before!

The world was a vast hunting-ground for God. You had but to be bold and alert, to watch for every track, to be quick as a flash in gauging the moment to attack as well as to be on your guard; you had to learn to have every expression, every inflection of your voice, every laugh and every gesture as completely under your control as any actor or diplomat; and, like a gambler, you had to be willing to stake your all on a single card. . . . Yes, it was like a glorious, exhilarating game in which you were constantly pledging your life, your honour and your safety to win immortal souls, the souls of your brothers and sisters in Christ. What a joy it was, with a cool head, but your heart aglow, and thrilling to your finger-tips with excitement, to embark on such an adventure, on the many alluring, secret adventures of that royal chase. It was sometimes like that strange electric current in the air to which your blood and your nerves respond by the feverish unrest that heralds the breaking of a storm.

*　　*　　*　　*　　*

She had no regrets for her lost dreams, her pious acquaintances noted with disapproval; she had soon learnt to forget. Her eyes, once misty with dreams, were now bright and keen as steel. There was about her an extraordinary atmosphere of buoyancy when she approached you, erect and striding firmly as though to an attack, with her head held high like a fiery steed. The delicate flower-like beauty of other days had undergone a strange process of transmutation. Diana of the chase! a Dutch painter had cried, when he glimpsed her one night at a garden fete rushing past beneath the myriad fairy lights at the head of a bevy of girls; and he was not so wrong either. To be sure, he did not know—nobody knew—that her dress of heavy crimson velvet with its wide Vandyck collar concealed a hairshirt which, together with the knotted leather discipline with which she scourged herself almost every night, was the sole memento she had brought away with her from the Convent of St. Clare. Not even her own family knew that after her return late of nights from an endless round of festivities, with the pages of her cavaliers tripping along beside her sedan-chair with their dancing lights, Mary knelt, dead tired as she was, on the bare floor for many a long hour in the darkness, and prayed and prayed, until she finally fell asleep where she knelt with her head on the bed.

But the poor quarters of the city knew her, too. Often enough of a night, with a shawl over her head and in the humble garb of a serving-maid, she might be seen flitting through the streets in quest of those hunted confessors of the faith who had escaped from prison, of outlaws who had crept to some hiding-place to die, or of the helpless and untended sick, the old people and the children of the family of the faith. She knew all the hovels and squalid dens over-run with rats and vermin from which the Plague was to stalk some few years thence, the water-side taverns with their crowds of soldiers, cripples, gipsies, prostitutes, spies and smugglers. Everywhere there were Catholics amongst them,

Catholics who had long forgotten they had ever been Catholics (or, haply, preferred to forget it), but brothers and sisters, all the same, for whom you would be called to give an account on the great Day of Reckoning, when the Divine summons would come, and you would surely not wish to answer in the words of Cain.

To such haunts she guided the steps of disguised priests, having first prepared the way—the general confession after twenty years, baptism of adults, the return of the lapsed, Extreme Unction, a marriage service long over-due—for often enough, the Father had to ride on the same night, consequently one rite had to follow the other with as little delay as possible. To the valiant-hearted girl he then entrusted the care of his new converts, of the sheep who had returned to the fold, the sick, and children in need of instruction. Full of enterprise and unflagging zeal, Mary took on everything as it came; for her enough was never enough. Soon she had so many charges that she found it impossible to remember all their names; but she knew them by sight, and that sufficed. Many a time she would intercept a wink or a quiet nod when on the following day, as though nothing had happened, she drove or rode in gallant company down the crowded Strand, and on such occasions she would return the covert greeting with an innocent and puzzled little smile.

Soon she no longer went her ways alone—neither those secret dangerous ways by the waterside, nor those others, none the less dangerous, exposed to the gaze of every eye at court or in the reception-rooms of the great; the bevy of young beauties whom the painter had likened to nymphs of Diana rallied ever more closely around her—at first, merely as young girls are wont to attach themselves to one whom they hold in romantic veneration, never weary of gazing at her, secretly envying the glance or the chance word she bestowed on another, and therefore eternally on her track, sueing and envious by turns. Presently, however, with the jubilant thrill of the born leader, she recognized what was beginning to glow in those young hearts and to flame into life. One after the other, she singled them out for heart-to-heart talks, knew then that it was fire of her fire, reflected but dimly as yet in the souls of those young dreamers, and by an appeal that was at once an entreaty and a command, stirred it to a flame, making them her willing slaves with the power of her sweet enchantment. Then she set to work to bring about a better understanding amongst them all, to ensure that the baneful element of jealousy, which flourishes best in an atmosphere of watchful, suspicious tension and tortured uncertainty, should be transformed into readiness pure and simple for a greater, finer bond, in a frank comradeship of arms, full of pride one in the other since each and every one was honoured by her implicit belief in them. There were secret meetings by candlelight in Mary's chamber, with the doors and windows securely bolted and barred, whilst she discoursed to them of the Kingdom of God, of the Church's hour of need, of how different things were in a Catholic country and of what it meant to lead a spiritual life.

One night they were again assembled thus. The fire clicked softly on the hearth, while over the world outside hung a thick brown November fog, through which each girl had groped her way alone, for the house had already begun to arouse the interest of observant watchers. The little circle was complete: Mary and her sister Barbara, the only one of the family who had discovered the elder girl's secret; Mary Poyntz, but sixteen years of age, but already surpassing all the others in her courageous frankness of speech and shrewdness of judgment (that night, though, that impulsive ardent spirit of hers was unusually subdued, for only the previous day she had given back his ring to her cousin and betrothed for the love of a heavenly Bridegroom and her heart was still weary and a little sore after the victory won); blond Winefrid Wigmore, very quiet and absolutely trustworthy, Mary's one really confidential friend; Susanna Rookwood, the court lady, getting on for thirty now, like Jane Browne, matter-of-fact and well versed in the ways of the world, but now aflame with the same consuming passion; Catherine Smith, who could ride like the devil and dance like an Italian, immune as any lad to dangers and fatigues.

That night, Mary felt vaguely puzzled as she glanced around her at the familiar circle—what was the matter with them all? Their faces were flushed, and they whispered amongst themselves and nudged one another with an occasional meaning glance in her direction, for all the world like so many school-girls. Then Mary Poyntz suddenly took heart and began: "Mary, we just wanted to tell you—you've got to hear it some time, so why not now—that we've decided—well, that you're never going to be rid of us again. We six simply mean to stick to you, go where you will. We want to obey you as you obeyed your Superior at St. Omer. All we possess is at your disposal—oh yes, we've already talked it over with our fathers—and if you go abroad, we intend to go too. If, however, you should enter some religious order, you'll just have to take all of us along with you, for we belong together; so now you know!"

At first Mary was incapable of uttering a single word,

and could only gaze at each one in turn in blank amazement. Then she closed her eyes, like one overwhelmed by a great shock or a great happiness, and trying to collect her thoughts. At that moment, her soul in a swift flight seemed to cover the space, not only of the last three years, but of hundreds of years to come. Once more, she saw herself amongst the dykes and floating gardens on the highroad to Gravelines with Sister Jacqueline at her side. They had put down their heavy loads for a moment to rest; the wind came in great salt gusts over the low-lying land, and she met it with outstretched arms. And then Sister Jacqueline had asked: "Are you homesick, Sister?" And Mary still heard herself saying: "No . . . there are many fingers tapping at my heart like prisoners sending messages to one another—only as yet I don't understand what they are trying to say."

Now she understood what then for one brief moment had passed through her soul as though in some half-waking dream. She opened her eyes, smiled at her companions and said: "Good—then let us sail with the next ship for St. Omer, buy a house there and assemble all the little girls of our kinsfolk that are within reach —and the next generation of Englishwomen shall be Catholics, reared on Catholic soil."

*   *   *   *   *

And thus we next find them in a rambling old house in the Grosse Rue at St. Omer—the six English Ladies —though there were soon to be more of them, for Barbara Babthorpe, the same Barbara who as a child had listened with Mary to Margaret Garrett's convent reminiscences, soon managed to have her way and join them, so that all Lady Grace's common-sense and eloquence in this case proved of no avail. In addition, each girl brought with her a faithful serving-maid, whom she had won over for the same way of life. Two years later, the new community already numbered fifty.

By that time, the residents of the little town had grown accustomed to see a long procession wending its way every morning through their streets to the cathedral or to St. Bertin's or, on the days of the great pilgrimages, to the neighbouring sanctuary of Notre Dame des Miracles. It was headed by the Sisters in their long black gowns and white linen coifs beneath a black silk veil, much the same attire, in fact, as that affected by widowed ladies of gentle birth. Then came the more colourful crowd of the English boarders, walking two and two in a most impressive silence, broken here and there, to be sure, by an occasional whisper or a suppressed giggle. People had also grown accustomed to see the coaches and litters of ecclesiastical dignitaries, of ambassadors at the court of Brussels, or of distinguished *émigrées* lined up before the gateway surmounted by the statue of St. George, whilst their occupants were being shown over the establishment or called to make inquiries after the health of the young daughters of some of England's most ancient and noble families. They were not even gossiped about unduly, for these strange "English Ladies," as everyone called them, had proved a very real blessing to the little town. Not only did they give instruction to their aristocratic boarders, but they had also opened a day-school where the little girls of the poorer classes were taught reading, writing and sewing for the love of God, something hitherto unprecedented in those parts. Winefrid Wigmore, who could speak five languages, gave the lessons in French and

H

Flemish, and children who showed any special aptitude were also taught English and were given an opportunity to practise it with the boarders. And all the pupils educated at the new school distinguished themselves from all others by their model behaviour and pretty manners, for all the world as though they were ladies to the manner born.

Those who discussed the English Ladies most were the clergy of the town—and the nuns of its innumerable convents. Of course, it was most praiseworthy that these young women were so full of zeal for all the works of Christian charity, more especially for the education of the young. And certainly you heard nothihg but what was edifying concerning the private lives of the new community. It hardly seemed credible that persons who, after all, were living in the world could lead such saintly lives. They rose early, they slept on straw, they even had no more than a single meal a day, just like the Poor Clares—which usage, no doubt, the Foundress had retained since her days as a novice in that convent— and yet these strange Sisters were all of noble lineage. The rooms in which they lived were practically bare, as like the cells of a real convent as made no difference. They also observed strict silence, and recited their prayers, and made their devotions in community.

Now, what were you to think of it all? They lived like religious of the strictest observance and yet were ordinary lay-folk, bound by no holy rule. They did not wear a habit, though the long line of them all in widow's garb—despite the fact that they were all unmarried—certainly made a curiously severe and nun-like impression. They recited Our Lady's Office, observed silence and fasting, something, after all, that only nuns did—and yet simultaneously they were carrying on the distracting business of running a school, which brought them day in, day out, in constant contact with lay-folk, municipal authorities and the parents of the children themselves. They went about the streets, too, quite unconcernedly, sometimes even alone, and accompanied their pupils to church, even on such days when every alley and the market-square were full of the noise and the bustle of the great pilgrimages. Now, how was all this compatible with the austere religious life which they were said to be leading?

The whole thing was a mass of contradictions, was neither fish nor flesh. Nobody knew what to make of it. If they felt they had a religious vocation and desired to lead an austere life to the glory of God and for the good of their souls, why did they not enter one of the excellent orders that again and again had received the full approval of Holy Church? Was there not in every street a convent what would welcome such devout aspirants to the religious life with open arms?

If, on the other hand, they had no vocation and merely wished to devote themselves to the works of corporal mercy (and, as their zeal for instruction proved, of spiritual mercy, too), why within the privacy of their own four walls all these strange conventual practices which, for the matter of that, were already the talk of the town? People should know what they wanted; such inconsistency boded no good. It was quite enough already, some would then add (though not too loud), that the Jesuit Fathers had introduced a strange new mode of life quite unlike anything that had ever been known before—freer than the secular clergy, stricter than the old religious orders, elusive, audacious, an extraordinary power for the glory of the Church, to be sure, but all the same, just a trifle uncanny. But women—devout

young women! Was it perhaps just possible that the
house in the Grosse Rue was really intended to be the
nucleus of some new religious order? In that case, it
might be as well to investigate the matter betimes.

Mary suddenly found herself called upon to deal with
a positive spate of ecclesiastical visitors in black and
purple cassocks, even in a variety of religious habits.
Very erect, she sat on her backless chair, her hands lightly
clasped in her lap, her eyes cast down, whilst they
interrogated her in a kindly paternal way about her aims
and future plans. Did she not feel drawn to any of the
older orders? Had she not, perhaps, been overmuch
and, maybe, too easily discouraged by the failure of her
early experiment at the Convent of the Poor Clares?
Had she carefully perused the Life of the Holy Mother
St. Teresa? Or the Rule of the Holy Father St. Benedict?
Whether any of her Sisters had shown any leanings
towards this order or that, and whether she was aware
that in such an event she was bound in conscience to
do nothing to oppose the call of God and of His holy
saints? Did she consider her rule of life superior to those
of the old religious orders?

Very civilly and modestly she told them that she was
acquainted with the other orders and entertained for
them the deepest respect, that the Lord, however, had
not yet made manifest His will to her and that she must
perforce wait on His pleasure. She was not aware that
any of her Sisters had any other religious vocation, but,
on the other hand, in the course of the last two and a half
years, fourteen of the senior pupils had entered Benedictine Convents in Brussels, Antwerp, and other centres.

The clerical gentlemen then asked to be permitted to
put one more question: was she likewise conversant with
the canons of the Holy Council of Trent, or was it just

possible that, owing to the unhappy conditions then obtaining in England, they had unfortunately never been brought to her notice, more particularly those concerning a more rigorous observance of the enclosure in women's convents and the episcopal jurisdiction over same? So many grave errors regarding a so-called universal sacerdocy were current amongst lay-folk, more particularly in countries where heresy had gained the upper hand, and amongst these errors there were gross misconceptions regarding the God-ordained nature and status of women in the Catholic community, so that the guardians of the purity of Catholic doctrine had to be extremely vigilant. He begged the good Sisters to pray for the extirpation of such heresies and to admonish their pupils most urgently to be on their guard against them.

Mary duly promised and accompanied her visitor with every courtesy to the gate. On arriving there, she asked him so simply and unaffectedly to pray that God would enlighten her that his stern eyes met hers with a swift look of suspicion, then, almost scared by such cheerful humility, he averted them hastily and departed more hurriedly than he had come.

Mary, however, slowly mounted the stairs to the parlour, saying with a shake of her head to her faithful Winefrid, who gentle and quiet as usual, though looking rather pale, was awaiting her at the door: "Winnie, now just imagine what would happen if they knew what we've been up to in England!" Whereupon both found relief for their feelings in a hearty peal of laughter.

*　　*　　*　　*　　*

Ah, England! Not so very long before the above-recorded interview, Mary had paid her native country another visit. Her little community at Spitalfields had been doing good work. Two priests were now in permanent residence and as yet no arrests had been made. This reign of peace, however, appeared to have been but the lull before the storm. Spies were on their tracks, and they had been obliged to change their lodgings several times. Mary found herself continually besieged by all manner of people seeking her help—Catholics and heretics, confessors and renegades—who had been secretly apprised of her coming and who now fought for the privilege of having a few words with her. This time her chief solicitude were the humble Catholics of the lower orders, who found greater difficulty in attending mass, had much to suffer from brute force, and were, in the main, more easily intimidated.

Oh, those nights passed in stables and servants' quarters amongst dog-tired drowsy men who smelt of sweat and brandy, but who listened to her open-mouthed and recited the rosary with her like little children . . . then the return home creeping close to walls and hedges accompanied by a faithful dog and lighted by the milk-white cascade of stars of a midsummer night! Was there anything more wonderful in the whole wide world?

And then the meetings with her Sisters, who arrived in the strangest attire, for all the world as though it were Carnival, all still a little breathless and shaken from their latest adventures, from which they had just managed to emerge by the very skin of their teeth, all bubbling over with an almost daredevil zest in the great gamble of life and death. And yet it was no vain spirit of bravado that danced in their eyes, for behind it all there was that unspoken, beckoning hope, shared by all, yet never mentioned: the secret longing to be found worthy of the supreme sacrifice, so that, as ever in the past, from the blood of victims new life might spring. . . .

This was better than the polite covert crossing of rapiers in the parlour of St. Omer, better than the weary campaign with goose-quills and sealing-wax against distrustful friends and patrons, jealously susceptible to every shade in your voice, ever-ready to lend a willing ear to the spiteful insinuations of the narrow-minded and ill-disposed.

The following autumn brought an epidemic of measles which spread like wildfire amongst day-girls and boarders alike. While nursing the others, Mary herself fell a victim and for a time hovered between life and death. Her physicians, at the end of their resources, shook their heads gravely, and the Lord Abbot of St. Bertin brought her the Viaticum. In this dire extremity the whole community vowed to make a pilgrimage on foot through Flanders and Brabant, and another fifteen miles beyond Louvain, to the miraculous image of Our Lady of Montaigu, whose new church had been built by the Archduchess Isabella. Winefrid Wigmore remained behind to nurse the sick Mother.

Passing through the strangely deserted and silent rooms adjacent to the sick-chamber she suddenly heard Mary talking to herself, and, thinking that the fever had risen again, she softly opened the door. Mary sat erect in her bed, looking strangely white and cool, and a light shone in her eyes that made Winefrid shudder: Was it already the glory of the Lord those eyes beheld?

The sick woman, however, motioned her to approach, and as she sank trembling on her knees beside the bed, Mary embraced her with a tempestuous affection quite unlike herself. "Win," she cried, "let us thank the

Lord: now I know the road we have to follow!—No, I'm not a bit feverish: listen, listen very attentively, so that one day you will be able to swear that in the self-same hour I told it you thus and in no other terms. Listen. Just now, I was lying feeling quite peaceful and comfortable, for the first time free from headache and that sense of numbness, as though my soul had been plunged into cool water. Then all of a sudden, in the midst of this feeling of quiet and lucidity, I heard the words—clearly, though only in the spirit, not by sound of voice: *Take the same of the Society. Father General will never permit it. Go to him.* The message was just as clear as that other one on the Feast of Saint Athanasius telling me I was to leave the convent. The import of the words must be taken literally; not a syllable may be added or altered. In other words, we are to adopt the rule of the Jesuits both in matter and manner, as far as is possible for us as women to do."

Then, with a deep sigh of relief, she added: "Now everything is in order as far as I am concerned; it only remains for me, in my turn, to remain faithful to the grace of God."

"And how do you propose to carry this out?" Winefrid timidly demurred.

"That the Lord must do. It will not be easy, but— O Win, do you realize what it means suddenly to see your path clearly before you! I firmly believe that at this very moment I am already quite a different being. Now I am going to get well again, too!"

She lay down on her side and the next moment was asleep, her lips parted in a happy smile.

Winefrid tiptoed softly from the room.

       *   *   *   *   *

Such an order was certainly not easy to carry out. Father Lee, who from the foundation of the Institute had faithfully guided its destinies and acted as its spiritual director, and to whom Mary was further bound by a vow of obedience, ordered her peremptorily and with the full weight of his authority to put the idea entirely out of her head. Could God be against God? Mary was quick to perceive that in this instance Father Lee's decision was prompted by the fear of annoying developments rather than by any special illumination from on high, so she waited patiently and with all due respect until he was calmer and broached the subject of his own accord.

To Winefrid she merely opined that God had certainly apportioned physical and moral courage amongst the sexes in a marvellous way, seeing that to every ten men who could face naked steel, a wild horse or a band of robbers without blenching, there was not a single one capable of holding his own against a weeping woman, a scold or an angry superior. *His* Superiors, said Father Lee, had made up their minds that the whole idea was obviously a temptation of the Evil One.

"Know," was Mary's reply, gently spoken, though there was a glint of battle in her eye, "that the Jews also called Our Lord Himself a sinner and said He had a devil."

But St. Ignatius had expressly forbidden his sons to occupy themselves with the direction of sisterhoods.

"That is why I, and not you, have received this charge," said Mary very politely, adding that, after his unfortunate experience with Donna Isabella, the Saint's decision was quite comprehensible, without, on the other hand, anyone being bound to regard it in the light of a higher revelation.

The way of life, and independence in exercising authority, were unsuitable for women, said Father Lee.

Mary almost lost patience. Why did men always first have to build up a pompous theory supported by weighty arguments and fortified with solemn conclusions, instead of simply opening their eyes and looking facts in the face! Could he not see for himself how extremely well this "way of life" suited them all? She, too, had some experience of convents and she was amazed herself to see how peaceably, precisely her own little community got on together. And as to the impossible form of government—the Father knew very well that ever since Mary's illness, Barbara Babthorpe had had the management of the entire establishment, in addition to that of the novices who had long been her special charge, therefore was Superior of the House in all but name. For all that, Mary herself had no intention of allowing the reins of government to pass out of her hands. Thus, they already had, as a matter of actual fact, the allegedly impracticable form of administration, namely that a Mother General was managing the affairs of the House, in conjunction with Superiors subordinate to herself—for as soon as the Liége house, for which they were now in negotiations, was opened, it, in its turn, would also need just such another Superior, who would be subject to the Mother House. What was there then "impracticable" or fantastic in such an arrangement? It had all been tried out just like the other functions of Procuratress, House Mistress, the teaching staff, door-keeper, and the rest. That she was unable to bind herself to any specific habit, much less to enclosure, as long as the English Mission was her chief concern, he knew as well as she did. That she must reserve for herself the right to dismiss insubordinate or incapable members, even though they had already made their profession, was all the more necessary for the dangerous campaign they were undertaking, since its success depended entirely on the absolutely trustworthy character of each individual member. And these were the famous unprecedented innovations—every single one perfectly reasonable and, in fact, necessitated by the type of work they were doing—how did he suggest, then, that it should else be done?

"You'd better write to Rome," said Father Lee, and retired in good order.

       *   *   *   *   *

And write Mary did—pages and pages of elegant Latin forming an impressive Memorial, bound in silk and hung with many seals, were dispatched to Rome in the baggage of an English agent. That was in January, 1616. Shortly before, Father Lee had died at Dunkirk. Towards the end he had done everything in his power to inspire Mary with renewed courage—the Caraffa Pope was an ardent promoter of all activities connected with the Counter-Reform; many new religious orders had come into being or were prospering under his pontificate, thus, the Lazarist Fathers, the Brothers of Christian Doctrine, the priestly family of St. Philipp Neri, in addition to new Congregations of women such as the devout Ladies of the Visitation, founded by Monsignore Francis, Bishop of Geneva, in conjunction with Madame de Chantal, the Sisters of the Annunciation, and many others. He forgot to add that at first Mgr. de Sales had had much the same aims in view as Mary herself, but that in the battle for freedom from enclosure he had been decidedly worsted.

A gracious reply was received through Cardinal Lanzeolotti. Bishop Blaise was to afford all the assistance in his power to the devout English Ladies by his protection and blessing. The Holy See would consider the matter of confirming the new Institute "if as we trust, the harvest of good works shall have ripened more abundantly."

At St. Omer everything pursued its normal trend. Imperceptibly the Franciscan character of the community, with its grinding poverty and corporal austerity had merged into the Ignatian school of piety. The following year brought the opening of a new foundation at Liége in response to the urgent and personal appeal of a number of good Catholic ladies of that city. Ferdinand, the Prince Bishop, a brother of the Elector of Bavaria, wrote them some very gracious letters, authorizing the Sisters to build a College, Church and school.

But the buzzing of poisonous wasps in England was beginning to make itself heard also in Rome. In the Chancellery of the Holy Office, the files of documents dealing with the "Wardesses or Jesuitesses, who gad about the world with the object of preaching the Gospel to persons of their own sex," were swelling to imposing dimensions.

Mary found herself once more obliged to go to England in order to discover the identity of her enemies and to put new heart into her faithful adherents. The state of affairs in England had grown steadily worse and was now more uncertain than ever. James I was playing a game of his own based on controversial arguments and theological subtleties instead of deciding one way or the other. One day, the whisper would go the round in all the Catholic embassies that His Majesty had advanced the opinion in the circle of his intimates that he, personally, held Rome to be the Mother of all Churches and the Supreme Bishop, the Pope, as her Head.

The following day, the unspeakable fear for the safety of his precious life, which ever since the Gunpowder Plot, had haunted him like a nightmare, would drive him to the devising of yet more penal laws against his Catholic subjects in order that the tidings of the signal triumphs of the Counter-Reform in France and Spain should not encourage them to make a sudden attack on the throne. And to-day, to-morrow and the day after to-morrow the royal coffers were always badly in need of money, and recusants paid honourably and unflinchingly, even though they were nigh unto bursting with secret rage. The spy industry was doing exceedingly well; its members called themselves Crown Agents, which somehow seemed to make their thirty pieces of silver a trifle cleaner.

The "Great Game" of the gallant-hearted young women of Spitalfields had become more dangerous than ever. Their eyes no longer sparkled so mettlesomely, and when they met, they no longer discussed the dangers they had passed, having no desire to add to one another's burdens. To Mary, their faces seemed to have grown harder, more dogged; even their laughter had a touch of grimness and their eyes were very watchful. The eternal play-acting palled in the end. The yellow Parisian ruffs, more sensational than ever, about which a pious sleuth immediately transmitted a hasty report to Rome, the gleaming taffetas, the slashed and puffed sleeves, the folds of which could be made to serve as *caches* for secret missives, had now something of that spectral quality that clothes the masqueraders in a Dance of Death. Everybody seemed to have two faces; you never knew when you attended a social affair whether the cavalier opposite in scarlet satin, with the tuft on his chin and the lovelocks curling over his lace collar, who was looking

at you in such a strange furtive way, was not going to
draw his sword all of a sudden and summon his myrmidons in the King's name—or whether he was simply
waiting for an opportunity to whisper under cover of
the airs and graces of a court gallant: "I'm Father
Ingleby from Calais and should like to know whether
you can get in touch with penitents before to-night."

You never knew whether the silken comfit-box left
at the door after nightfall by some unknown messenger,
contained poison or whether it was an even more
poisonous attempt on the part of some Catholic spy to
besmirch the reputation of the hated "Jesuitesses"
("... they do secretly receive gifts from gentlemen of
high estate ..."), whether, as was recorded in the
accompanying sonnet, some unknown had really succumbed to the witchery of her beautiful eyes, someone
who had taken the ruff and the play with the fan at
their face value—or whether at the bottom of the
perfumed casket some odd scrap of paper contained a
heart-rending appeal indited in lemon juice, which
became visible only when held over a candle-flame:
"My husband who apostatized last year, has been thrown
from his horse and would fain be reconciled with the
Church. . . . Hasten, and for the love of God, bring a
priest with you; he has but a few short hours to live."

They were now living at Knightsbridge in the house
of a Protestant friend, and the diligent agent who dispatched such lengthy epistles to Rome was now able
to report that aforesaid young women were not only
living in the house of a heretic but also stole off of nights
through the park, marvellously attired, to the belvedere,
whiles hired minstrels posted at the gate and below the
windows drowned with the noise of their serenades every
sound that emerged from the heathen temple.

The Secretary of the Holy Office perused these reports with a darkening brow, underscored the most scandalous passages with red pencil and laid them to a formidably swelling pile.

But nobody wrote to Rome to say how many lost ones had been found again, how many strayed and despairing souls as well as staunch but weary fighters, on such nights were reconciled, consoled, and strengthened with the Body of the Lord in that little bower of roses. Nobody dreamt of reporting that the recusants, more especially the women, had suddenly risen to double the number, and that in the opinion of the Archbishop of Canterbury, Mary Ward was "the Great Evil" and did more harm than half a dozen Jesuits.

Having heard of his interest in her person, rather flattering albeit disapproving, Mary decided one day to honour him with a visit and wagered her sisters that she would return safe and sound from the lion's den, a very spiritual and gentle lion to be sure. Her companions had lost the taste for such adventures, but Mary was not likely to be stopped by any objections they could offer. So two of them accompanied her as far as the gardens of Lambeth Palace, and the young gardener pruning the roses behind the yew hedges sympathetically assumed that the two young ladies were waiting for the arrival of some faithless swain, who had forgotten to keep his appointment, since they looked so extremely pale, paced up and down with tightly clenched fists, started at every footstep, and every now and again cast longing glances in the direction of the gate. He was decidedly taken aback, though positively relieved, when at last they flew into the arms of a tall laughing lady who swept along past his flower-beds with quick firm steps and was carried off by them in triumph.

"Unfortunately he was not at home," Mary told them, "but I left my name on one of his window-panes —a good thing I had the diamond ring with me. Now at least, he will know that I have been thinking of him too."

Her luck was almost uncanny—decidedly uncanny, said her enemies, and whispered things that were best not said aloud; she stood under God's special protection, asserted her friends. Even when finally she was taken prisoner, the charm continued to work, cowed her guards, who, half sheepish, half proud, stood on guard at her door, gave themselves the most insufferable airs when she gave them a pleasant word, and practically effaced themselves when their presence was deemed superfluous, though they were under orders not to leave her cell. They even administered a sound thrashing to one of their number when he came off duty for having helped himself to her belongings, as they were wont to do with other prisoners; after which chastisement an emissary was dispatched who, blushing furiously, returned the crystal reliquary to its rightful owner. During her second term of imprisonment at the Guildhall, sentence of death was passed upon her, but a judicious greasing of palms on the part of her friends once more opened her prison doors.

"I thought as much," said Mary to Susan Rookwood, who came to meet her at the prison gate and at the sight of her wan sad smile hardly knew whether to congratulate her or not on her escape. "The whole time, I was trying to prepare myself for death and banish all thoughts of our work like a swarm of chickens from the threshold—but I knew I didn't believe it myself that the end was in sight, and however much I blush to think of it, I told myself that I could not be spared yet awhile, so important I still am in my own sight. So, you see, I'm not ripe for martyrdom yet."

"It may be a greater privilege to assist souls on their path to heaven than oneself to suffer the martyr's death," said Susan softly.

*　　*　　*　　*　　*

At Liége, she found a house divided against itself. Sister Praxedes, the little peasant girl from the Ardennes, a curious mixture of silent introspection and sudden fierce ardours, announced that she had had celestial visions and dreams in which Mary had been exposed as a dangerous fanatic and herself had been appointed in her stead for the carrying on of her work. The Fathers of the English College, who knew of her terrible penances and her nights spent in prayer, deemed her to be a saint; half the Convent itself was ranged on her side.

Mary, fresh from an English prison, was received in silence. Bleak faces and furtive looks confronted her, feverish whispering arose directly her back was turned, and died down sullenly when she inquired what it meant.

Ah, how much harder was the battle against disgust and contempt of such as these and against one's own mortal weariness than that against English judges and guards! It was far easier to argue with Calvinistic ministers, sober-minded, learned men, than to deal with the wild feverish rantings of the visionary in which Mary's keen intuition, with a touch of genuine physical revulsion, seemed to sense the very odour of corruption. But then, was it not sheer pride and obstinacy to consider her own self as indispensable? Was it not just possible that God had chosen the weak vessel, the one despised of men, as His instrument? What need had

I

God of her accomplishments? "Thou art my God, for Thou hast no need of the work of my hands," Mary prayed in that dark hour; "Thou canst work what Thou wilt and through whom Thou wilt—but, alas! when I say this, it is but with my lips, and my heart cries against it. . . . Thou must needs let me die, my Lord and God, before my work is finished, so that at last I be made to grasp that Thou hast no need of me."

A great confidence filled her whole soul. That prayer was not a gesture, it really rose from the deepest depths of her heart. Now she could take up the battle once more with a mind at peace. Praxedes was told to commit her proposed rule of life to paper, as meticulously as though she were already alone in the world with her responsibilities, just as though everything from now onward depended solely on her. She, Mary, would do the same, and the churchmen should decide in God's name which of the two documents bore the stamp of God. She herself would wholeheartedly submit herself to their decision.

"That was not wisely done," Barbara Babthorpe demurred, puckering her brow; "You know very well that the Fathers at the Jesuit College have been gulled by her stories—it is folly to ask those who do not wish us well to be our judges. Personally, I should have asked the Bishop at the very least to decide in the matter."

Mary merely smiled, but in such a way that Barbara immediately regretted that she had spoken. That same evening Praxedes announced that, owing to an indisposition, it had been impossible for her to commit anything to paper. During the night, the bell suddenly summoned the Convent to the bedside of a very sick woman who clung to Mary whimpering and implored the Sisters with heart-rending sobs and tears to assume, in the event of

her illness proving fatal, that all she had seen and heard
in her "visions" had been false.

The following morning, still horror-struck, but moved
even more profoundly by an adoring realization of the
Divine justice, Mary and Barbara held their watch
beside the dead.

The Praxedes affair was a clear warning that some
definite ecclesiastical approval was needed for their way
of life. The nuncio Albergati said much the same thing
when their new house was opened at Trèves. It was
sheer audacity to go on founding new communities in
such a state of uncertainty. Rome must speak the decisive
word. But the road to Rome by way of correspondence
and memorials was interminable, and the Lord Cardinals
and the Protonotaries had plenty of other things to
occupy them rather than to trouble themselves about a
few English Ladies in a Flemish provincial town. The
great frame of the German Empire was creaking in
every joint; war had now been raging for more than
four years, the League against the Union. The Turks,
too, were bestirring themselves once more. The courts
of Mantua and Toscana had failed to come to any
agreement; the French go-betweens were not to be
trusted, and from the great mission fields in the New
World came the most disquieting and contradictory
reports, as if the old orders were fighting against the new.
And, as Mary had finally discovered, in the Vatican
itself there were certain personages who encouraged the
secret feud against her. They received many letters from
England, and yet there was not one amongst their
number who knew her personally.

"What shall we do?" asked Winefrid, somewhat
shaken in her sweet serenity.

"Go to Rome," said Mary, "see the Holy Father. No, I'm not crazed, Winnie, but I do realize that things cannot go on like this any longer. Do you imagine they even trouble to read our letters when every day they're receiving others, signed by people with distinguished names and addressed to all the leading prelates, with whom we are not even acquainted, nor our own good Fathers either for the matter of that? I pray you, hurry up and see what you can do to scrape enough together for our travelling expenses."

* * * * *

All this took time, and in the interim Pope Paul had died at Rome and, according to the Fathers at the College, Pope Gregory XV, who succeeded him, was old, sickly, irresolute and easily led by others; much depended on which party approached him first, for he would then stick to it with all an old man's obstinacy. God sent Mary yet another valuable ally in the person of the saintly Carmelite, Father Domenico di Gesù Maria, whose prayers had obtained the victory of the Imperial troops at the White Mountain near Prague, and who had recently been entrusted with yet another Papal mission from Rome to France. At Trèves he had been laid up with a severe chill, and Ferdinand, the Prince Bishop of Cologne, had insisted on keeping him at his court. So great were the crowds that flocked to the cell of the saintly friar that the door had to be taken off its hinges. The English Ladies had heard, of course, that he was on intimate terms of acquaintance with all the courts of Europe, from Cracow to Madrid, and from Brussels to Sicily. Every diplomat feared him, and devout ladies of royal blood would kneel on his threshold for the

privilege of hearing a few words from his own lips.
The Pope undertook nothing without his advice, and
could refuse him nothing: Our Lady, it was said, frequently appeared to him; he could read the souls of men
with one swift glance; he had been known to tax hardened
sinners with their secret sins; he could see into the
future, and he was believed immune against plague and
bullets.

It was a glad day for Mary when, with a somewhat
fluttering heart, she sought out the holy friar, and found
a little, tired, old man, whose face seemed nothing
more than two burning eyes that fixed her with a penetrating glance for a moment, then became kind and
twinkling as any grandfather's.

"Have you ever seen young ravens who have been
thrown out of their nest by their parents for presuming
to come into the world without any feathers?" he asked.
"Just such an ugly, callow raven baby, that nobody
wants to handle is your Institute at its present stage.
But its feathers will sprout all right in time. They'll
trample you underfoot, yes underfoot. . . ."

He went on to Brussels, where he heard Archduke
Albert's last confession of his little private sins and his
grave political ones; then came a letter for Mary telling
her to discuss her journey to Rome with the widowed
Archduchess. They met in her private closet in which
some fourteen years before, Mary had received the
authorization for the foundation of the English Convent
of the Poor Clares. Isabella had discarded her strings
of pearls and was attired in the brown habit of a Franciscan Tertiary. The double chin, however, was still in
evidence and had grown even more impressive with
the passage of the years. She opined that Mary did not
seem to get any older, also that she was still far too

handsome to embark on so long and perilous a journey, and extracted from her the promise that she would at least avail herself of the protection afforded by pilgrim's garb. Mary was given letters of safe conduct from King Philip and the Emperor Ferdinand, even a personal letter to the Pope from the Infanta herself. The old lady hung a reliquary round her neck and took leave of her with a motherly kiss, a mark of tenderness to which Mary had long been a stranger. And when at last, attended by the black and gold pages, she descended the great staircase, she seemed to see herself once more, a girl in a brown travelling cloak waiting at the sacristy door, and she felt her heart thrill as it had thrilled then, courageously, jubilantly, eager and ready for the next adventure. No, she really had no time to grow old.

And now the curtain was due to rise on the second act of the great struggle.

* * * * *

On October the twenty-first, the Feast of St. Ursula, Mary set out with her little caravan on the great journey: five women in brown cloaks, high-crowned black beaver hats and narrow ruffs, a long pilgrim's staff in their hands and a rosary wound round their waists like a girdle. Father Lee, a nephew of their late first friend, escorted them under the name of Mr. Tomson, then came an ancient raw-boned steed, loaded high with seven firmly corded valises and some sacks of provender, who trudged along submissively, led by the bridle by a tall blond lad with closely cropped hair. The latter's name was Robert Wright, and he was almost a romance in himself.

One day, Mary had found him awaiting her in the parlour, a young man of some twenty years, with long cavalier locks, immaculate lace collar and cuffs, very red about the ears and as bashful as a schoolboy. Did she recognize him? He was a cousin of hers on the Babthorpe side. He had been visiting relatives at the English College, and he had thought that he would very much like to have some part in the arduous heroic lot of the confessors of the faith. Unfortunately, he felt not the slightest vocation for the priesthood, and in any case, was no good at study.

Mary was about to administer some sound advice, when he interrupted her with a proposal of his own: perhaps the Institute needed a man-servant? In the troublous times in which they were living, a community of young ladies would be none the worse for having a man about the house. He could, for instance, ride with their letters, and escort the Sisters on their journeys, the roads just then, in war-time, being none too safe.

Mary laughed and shook her head. The idea was not a bad one, but what would "the world" say if the English Ladies were to acquire a young man as housemate?

"Hm," mused Robert Wright. Then, brightening: "But suppose you were to hire an ordinary servant— a handy man to chop wood for the kitchen, fetch the sacks of flour from the miller's and your boarders' baggage from the ship—now, nobody could possibly object to that."

"But we can't afford the wages of a serving-man," said Mary, somewhat puzzled. She shook her head again in sheer bewilderment when the young gallant, making her a deep obeisance, swept the floor with the plume of his hat, then vanished abruptly without another word.

But that same evening, he was back again, with his hair cropped short and attired in a brown leather doublet and clumsy Flemish sabots. From his height of six feet, he then announced to Mary: "My name from now onward is Jack Morris, and I am your most faithful and devoted servant who desires naught from you but his board and free lodging and the privilege of working for you until the end of his days."

And thus Robert Wright had his way.

*   *   *   *   *

Thus we find Jack Morris trudging along, bringing up the rear of the tiny caravan, chewing a blade of grass or whistling softly and cheerfully to himself. It was he who stabled the horse, sought some sort of accommodation in the very doubtful taverns along the highways, or, if far and near there were none to be found, built a great fire of an evening on the outskirts of some secluded copse in a misty valley, bright with autumnal tints, and helped to prepare the evening meal. When that was over, he would crouch close to the dying flame and mount guard for the night, his cocked pistol across his knee, the sword of other days, usually stowed away in the serving-man's baggage, beside him on the dank grass, and above him the infinite star-studded autumn sky. Beside him Father Lee lay close by the fire, like himself wrapped in a cloak and his weapon within reach, still turning over the pages of his Breviary. Beyond in the shelter of the copse, safeguarded against the chilling damp of the earth by a thick layer of fir-twigs and bracken, slept the five women, enveloped in their mantles and rugs. Not with one of the great seamen would Jack have changed places, neither with Drake nor with Raleigh,

the heroes of his boyhood. Infinitely more stirring was
that strange journey, half pilgrimage, half gipsy vaga-
bondage, from Brussels to Trèves, through Lorraine on
to Nancy, riding through the very midst of troops,
wherever they went, troops on foot and on horse, baggage trains, thundering columns of heavy wagons and
an endlessly swelling stream of fugitives. Then through
Alsace to the Rhine, leaving the sombre blue forests of
the Vosges behind them, down into the plain full of
empty orchards and deserted vineyards. From its steep
rock, the fortress of Breisach held guard over the river,
whilst as far as the eye could reach stretched the Rhine-
bruch, with great tracts of underwood along the river-
banks, stunted growth and marshy soil, where every
kind of outlaw sought refuge. Then, leaving the great
river on their left, the little company pushed on through
the Sundgau in the direction of Basle. In the proud city
of wealthy merchant princes, throned on its seven lofty
hills above the fine bridge to the Klaravorstadt, they
paused for a brief rest. Towering above the Rheinsprung
the Minster, built by the saintly Emperor Henry, was
now of the reformed faith. Zwingli's preachers passed
in and out of the Golden Portal and all that her own
English homeland had lost came back to Mary's mind
as of old as she stood before the mutilated statues in the
cloisters.

Then their road swung off south-east and climbed
upwards into the mountains. Glimpsed for the first
time, a fairy world loomed above the pilgrims, gleaming,
snow-white and blue as glass, with peaks of eternal ice.
On they went, past mountain torrents, lonely Alpine
huts and deserted pastures, past precipitous, rubble-
strewn screes, until, as far as eye could reach, there was
nothing to be seen but snow, and yet again snow, for

by now, All Saints had come and gone, and the holy
season of Advent was before the door.

The road grew worse and worse, slippery with ice or
buried in snowdrifts. St. Gotthard offered welcome
hospitality, but the poor old horse had gone hopelessly
lame and had to be left behind, and their valises were
now strapped to their own backs.

At last the Italian lakes spread beneath them and the
land began to grow green once more. After the infinite
solitudes of the mountains came swarming plains,
cities, and the busy highroad from Como to Milan, to
the tomb of San Carlo Borromeo. On they trudged,
through Tuscany to Piacenza, over Bologna to Ancona
to the sanctuary of Loreto, and the miraculous house of
Our Lady, once borne through the air on angels' hands.
One hundred and fifty miles had been added to their
long and arduous journey, so that they might seek consolation of the heavenly Mother in her chosen sanctuary.
But, kneeling there amongst the noisy crowd of pilgrims
who all around her were kissing the ground, weeping,
moving round the church on their knees and praying
aloud with their arms upraised, Mary felt a chill of fear,
such as she had never known before, surge in her heart,
which grew heavier and tenser throughout the whole of
that dreary winter's morn.

Amongst themselves, the Sisters wondered what had
come over their Mother. She had headed their start
in a buoyant mood. She had revelled in the radiant
wonders of God's beautiful earth, in rivers and rocks
and waterfalls, in the lonely valleys with their autumnal
riot of colours, in lost streams, in the rugged majesty of
lone trees, in distant glaciers, and the ever-recurring glory
of the sunsets. . . . Her voice rang out above all the others

as they marched along singing, or sang as they rested around their camp-fire, and often enough her irrepressible humour had helped them over the worst surprises that awaited them in their disreputable hostelries. And now she was pale and quiet, and spoke never a word the livelong day, never a word.

Silent and oppressed, they continued their journey through the marshes and Umbria. Everyone was foot-sore, everyone's shoes were hopelessly worn out. The food they bought on the way was stale and nasty, never before had the inns been so revoltingly dirty. Jack Morris looked like a vicious watch-dog turning rabid for lack of sleep, for in those disreputable dens of thieves, he hardly dared to stir from his lady's side, and passed the nights on her threshold with his back propped against the door. 'Twas not such things he minded, for riding on the high seas, in hot pursuit of Spanish galleons from Peru, he would scarce have met with less hardships. But that his lady, bravest of her sex (and fairest, too, he thought in his heart of hearts) should lapse into so oppres-sive and gloomy a silence, that seemed to cut her off from the whole world, was almost more than he could bear.

And Father Lee's reflections ran very much as follows: "Women are women, after all, and should not embark on exploits fit only for men."

But he knew better than to voice his feelings.

Then Mary Poyntz, who was marching ahead, sud-denly stopped short with a cry. Far below, above the twilight city towards which they were journeying, the mighty arc of a great dome rose against the Christmas stars; and they marvelled to themselves when Mary slowly sank on her knees and, prostrating herself, kissed the ground. When they had resumed their march, she whispered to Winefrid, so softly that nobody else could hear: "I have resigned all things to the will of the Apostles, and I know that what is before us will not be easy to bear."

On Christmas Eve they entered Rome. The city glittered with myriad lights; pilgrims from all nations poured through the squares; triumphal arches and garlands of green swayed from balcony to balcony. The procession, with the Pope in its midst, streamed singing and praying to the Lateran; prelates and guards, monks and gentiluomini, torchbearers, beggars, clerics, street arabs, horsemen, litters, coaches, thronged every street and alley, and all the bells of the Eternal City carolled and clamoured beneath the starry heavens. Nobody noticed the little group of dead-tired, silent pilgrims amongst those vast crowds. Before they sought a hostelry for the night, Mary went to the Gesù and spent two hours on her knees before the tomb of St. Ignatius.

They found accommodation near the Ponte Sisto, close to the English College. The next step was to present their credentials. The saintly Carmelite was back again in the Vatican and thanks to his good offices, Mary had not long to wait, for she was received in private audience already on the Feast of St. Stephen.

"God hath in good time provided for His Church," said the Pope graciously, bending his eyes with kindly interest on the English pilgrim kneeling at his feet. The work she was doing was most praiseworthy, and he was glad that so many noble ladies had rallied round her banner.

With sparkling eyes Mary returned to the inn. "Never could I have imagined it would be so easy," she told the Sisters. They, in their turn, told one another that not even the Pope had been proof against the spell of Mary's enchantment.

How little they knew of Rome!

*   *   *   *   *

After a few days, they carefully packed away their pilgrim's garb and resumed their habits: the white bandeau, and the long black silk mantle falling from the close-fitting cap to their feet. The inquisitive people of Rome, accustomed as they were to every variety of dress from every part of the earth, turbans and caftans, brown, black and yellow skins, stopped to stare in the streets with loud exclamations of surprise, clapped their hands, shook their heads, and almost ringed them in, whilst a swarm of children danced at their heels whenever they ventured out of doors. That was a bit too much— nuns, to all appearances, real nuns (for the bandeau was surely not part of a Carnival masquerade?) nuns who went alone and on foot through the streets, where no lady ventured without an escort, and even then, in a sedan-chair! They went to church carrying large prayer-books, these eccentric foreigners—ladies of rank, as you could see at a glance—took up their positions close to the rood-screen and apparently recited the Divine Office with the other religious—as only religious had a right to do. But in the streets, they did not, forsooth, modestly cast down their eyes, but in all innocence watched the busy life that was going on around them, sometimes even stopping outside a shop to ask the prices of the wares exposed for sale, and to talk to the children. It was really preposterous. Neither did they lodge at a convent, but at an ordinary hostelry, had their meals there (only once a day to be sure), and sang litanies behind closed doors. And to crown all they had a priest and a young serving-man, the latter attending them when they walked abroad like a page, carrying their prayer-books and fetching their meals. From what dark land of heresy might they have sprung, where, manifestly, nobody knew anything about the decorum due to the religious state?

Very soon Father Lee found himself quite unable to cope with the number of his callers, especially with the ecclesiastical ones. They pointed out to him that these extraordinary ladies were making themselves embarrassingly and absurdly conspicuous, that he, in his turn, had attracted the attention of the Holy Office of the Inquisition, and that the least that could be expected of him was to find some other lodging. . . .

Other ecclesiastics called on Mary and after long serious talks vowed with amazement and delight that here at last was something that they themselves had long considered to be an urgent need in feminine religious life, aye, something absolutely indispensable and thoroughly in keeping with the times; for nowadays a considerable number of holy women were resolved on a life dedicated to God and yet felt a strong urge for apostolic work in the world.

But precisely these same friends implored her not to jeopardize the whole future of her work by discussing and even parading its more debatable aspects in so unconcerned a way. Let her at least dispense with the bandeau as long as their Institute had not been officially recognized. Let them seek to win golden opinions by their school and missionary work and only by degrees come out into the open and say that they wanted the Institute to be confirmed as a religious order.

Mary's reply was to show them the Memorial that she had been dictating day and night to Winefrid and of which she had had numerous copies made. The Holy Father, she said, was entitled to have a clear idea of what she was after. In regard to the Holy See, she could not do otherwise than lay all her cards on the table. The Supreme Teacher and Pastor of God's Church had a right to know everything that the Holy Spirit had charged His most unworthy daughter to perform.

There it stood, beautifully inscribed:

"Humbly we beseech Your Holiness to confirm in us this our holy vocation by the pronouncement that henceforth we are religious . . . by taking this our whole society under Your special protection and by not permitting that the Bishops in their dioceses nor any other hath any legal power or jurisdiction over us."

"Have you never heard anything of Canon Law, Mother Mary?" asked the Father with a sigh. "Or of the Council of Trent? Or of the Canons of Reform pertaining to women's convents?"

"They need not trouble us," said Mary with a shrug. "The Holy Ghost is stronger than all that."

Winefrid knew that tiny straight furrow between her eyebrows and that rather too carefully controlled tone in her voice. Knew therefore that the good Father might just as well save his breath. He, too, understood and betook himself off betimes, sighing gently as he went: "Sancta simplicitas—against our protonotaries and secretaries, even the Holy Ghost, sit venia verbo, gets the worst of it."

He said the same thing again, only somewhat louder, when some days later the canonical discussions on the subject of the Memorial began in the chancelleries of the Holy City, and from that time onward went on without end.

The English Ladies were beginning to feel quite at home in Rome. They visited friends in other women's convents, two remaining as guests with the Oblates of the Torre dei Specchi, in whom they found a certain spiritual kinship. In the company of the pious ladies of this semi-conventual foundation, they visited sick persons and captives in prisons; they waited and waited in chancelleries and antechambers, in the parlours of convents, and amongst guards and chamberlains at the Vatican. By degrees it struck Mary that the manner of the various officials with whom she came in contact had grown perceptibly cooler, that the answers they gave her were curter and more and more evasive, that her requests for a further audience with the Holy Father were being simply ignored. What had happened?

"There are some who are working against us," said Winefrid sadly; "we have enemies whom we do not even know."

"We must discover what we stand accused of," said Barbara, "then we can refute their accusations."

But Mary, deeply pained, flew out: "What, have you so poor and so mean an opinion of the Holy Father? Do you imagine we should be condemned without as much as a hearing? Without being confronted with our accuser? O fie, fie! that you should think so basely of him who deserves our implicit childlike trust!"

Father Lee, however, went about looking like a shadow, hardly touched his food and lay long awake of nights. He knew a good deal more than he was at liberty to say. A fellow-countryman who had good friends in the Papal Chancelleries had told him in strict confidence that a very important document relating to the new Institute had been received from England. It bore the signatures of the deputy English Archbishop and of many priests well known in Rome as zealous and valiant confessors of the faith. Under seven separate headings, the Memorial apprised the Holy See of the most weighty arguments against this strange Institute, not in any spirit of hostility or animosity, but impelled by a sense of responsibility and anxiety for the integrity of the Catholic religion, which, thanks to this impossible Order, was labouring under a grave and quite unneces-. sary disadvantage. The General of the Society of Jesus, to which the English Virgins had attached themselves with so exclusive a preference, had also solemnly disclaimed them, had declined any responsibility for this foundation, which had come into being without either his knowledge or his will, and had, moreover, explicitly forbidden his Fathers to interest themselves in any special way in the spiritual and temporal affairs of these same Virgins. The Society of Jesus had, as it was, enemies in plenty and had to fight hard enough for its good name without associating itself with the crazy enterprises of a few devout, though eccentric women.

The heat of a Roman June brooded over the city of stone. There was an epidemic of small-pox, and Barbara Ward, the youngest of the little community fell a victim, and did not recover. Kind friends took her to the country to recuperate, but she returned home to die. In those hospitable homes, she had had an opportunity of hearing much that was being said in pious circles on the subject of Mary and her Sisters.

"Everything's so very different here," she said sadly, when Mary and Susan shared the night-watches beside her bed. "How can these people possibly realize how things are at home in England? How can they understand that we're so at odds amongst ourselves, that even the faithful do not trust one another? They asked me whether it was true that we exercised priestly functions, and preached in public places, whether in families, we

K

heard people's confessions and told them we were in a position to dispense absolution provided they were truly contrite. Only think, they actually asked me whether it were true that many of us were secretly married and concealed the fact only for fear of giving scandal. ... You don't know whether to laugh or to weep at such foolery."

One day Jack Morris returned home with a bad sword wound in his shoulder. For some days he was laid up with a high fever, but it was only Father Lee who ever heard that he had been involved in a furious broil with a Cardinal's man, who had jeered at him for his service of the "Apostolic Amazons" and the "galloping-girls of the Jesuits." But it was the worst of the whole bad business that these coarse nicknames were not coined by the Italian rabble, but were cited from letters that had been penned by English priests. The boy had administered a sound thrashing to certain of these loose-tongued knaves, and one of them had retaliated with a dagger—but who could get at the real culprit?

One day Mary said to her sister: "I cannot stand this any longer. Don't you feel, too, that the attitude towards us is getting steadily worse with every day? Let them put us to the test. We will ask permission to open a school so that they can watch us at work, here, there, and everywhere, and will thus be able to see with their own eyes what dark and dangerous tricks we are up to."

"There are only five of us," said Margaret Horde ruefully; "we really know hardly any Italian as yet—and Barbara ..."

"Barbara Babthorpe will have to leave Liége and come here," interposed Mary quickly, "she must bring two Sisters along with her and two lay Sisters to do the cooking and washing, so that the teachers do not have to wear themselves out with such things. Little Nelly from St. Omer—she'll soon get over her silly fancies once she's here. And it will be months before they do get here. In the meantime, we'll get the Sisters of the Torre dei Specchi to teach us Italian."

That same night, the letter was already speeding on its way to the north. Amongst the letters that went with the same courier was one from Mr. John Bennett, agent of the English clergy, in which he wrote home to his Bishop: "The Jesuitesses are plying their business here in secret. . . . I am, however, given to understand that they will never be approved, unless with enclosure. All serious-minded persons whom I have heard discussing the matter at this court deem the whole business to be utter foolishness. . . ."

In winter the new Sisters arrived. Soon a big school had been started. They gathered together their little girls wherever they could find them, just as the Fathers of the religious schools had done with their boys, and after the children had overcome their first shyness of the foreign ladies, the school soon filled as though by magic.

"Five and twenty spies are constantly watching us," said Mary to her sister Barbara, whose sick-room had become an oasis of peace and consolation in the busy house. "Cardinal Mellino told me as much himself. We are living just as though we were in a glass house. Every word we utter the children have to report at home; everybody knows what we have for dinner and how much our meals cost, how much linen each one of us has, and who comes to the parlour. . . . But it *is* a good thing that we have naught to conceal."

Naught save her own unspeakable anxiety for the

beloved invalid—naught save her unspeakable weariness and the tears that flowed so freely in the lonely watches of the night. For Barbara had now but a few more days to live, and Mary was fully aware of it, in spite of all the prayers and Holy Masses with which the heavens were being stormed in other convents where they had friends, in spite of the great candle that burnt before the tomb of St. Ignatius. In the Casa Professa of Al Gesù, the dread Father General had a notice put up in the sacristy asking all Fathers to remember her before the altar. Mary knew that this meant a victory in yet another quarter, but the thought brought her no consolation. Ah, why had she taken her little sister, the youngest and most delicate of them all, on that terrible journey? Was this her punishment? How could she ever hope to justify herself, should God one day permit her to meet her parents again? The many cousins and nephews of the Sisters who were studying at the English College in Rome sent respectful messages of sympathy and promises of prayer. The pupils brought baskets of flowers and fruit.

On January 25th of the new year, Barbara died. Mary sent the others out of the room, then washed and clothed the body of her sister with her own hands. To her it seemed, somehow, not a sad, but a strangely solemn rite, as though what she had before her was something a good deal more than the dead body of her little sister. It was only when she was dictating to Margaret the letters craving the prayers of her priestly friends that it suddenly struck her that with her sister she had buried, finally and irrevocably, her own youth, that bit of England and childhood that in Barbara's chubby cheerful face had been so inexpressibly dear to her.

The number of their friends was again increasing. The

school of the English Ladies had proved a success, and the spies had become propagandists. The German Cardinal von Hohenzollern, who had made Mary's acquaintance when he was a Canon at Cologne, openly championed her cause. Cardinal Trescio, the austere Franciscan Tertiary, Archbishop of Salerno, and Cardinal Gimnasio, a friend of the saintly Carmelite Domenico, declared themselves her friends. Cardinal Bandino, President of the Holy Congregation and protector of the English clergy, and one who therefore knew best what accusations had been levelled against her, told a friend one day that, were it not derogatory to his priestly dignity, he would long have cast himself at her feet to ask her blessing.

Nevertheless, Mary found the atmosphere in Rome too stifling for the free development of her work. She longed to be away from the vigilance of friends and foes, from the eternal watchfulness of curious eyes, from the ceaseless torrent of well-meant but useless advice. At Naples, the residence of the Spanish Viceroy and of Archbishop Caraffa, two friends of the staunch-hearted old Archduchess Isabella, very different results, she felt, might be achieved.

*   *   *   *   *

Soon they were off again on another long journey. This time there were only four of them: Mary, Winefrid, and their two faithful paladins. It was May, not the shy, fragrant, green and white May of their homeland, but the torrid Roman summer with terrible thunderstorms, white-hot dust on the hard roads, and poisonous vapours over marshy land. A few scudi was all they had with them, and this time it was a decrepit old ass and not a horse, that patiently trudged along, bringing up the rear. But when the City, the holy, unholy City, had slipped away behind them in a long trailing cloud of dust, and a mighty wind, blowing from mountains invisible as yet, exultingly swooped down upon them, they suddenly stopped short, as though at a word of command, looked at one another, then burst into a hearty peal of laughter, and simply had to link hands for a moment like children. And Jack was whistling again, whistling the livelong day, a thing he had not done for some eighteen months past.

Two hundred miles in the burning heat of early summer, foul water, even fouler inns, sore feet, inflamed eyes, the constant peril of bandits and of troops of every nationality and race: what matter, when once more you had a clear free goal before you, when after an agonizing period of close confinement, you could move freely and stretch your limbs again? But by the time they reached Naples, Mary was in a fairly bad way; her teeth were chattering, she shivered and burnt by turns in a high fever. The little house promised them by a Roman friend was found to consist solely of four walls and a roof sadly in need of repair; they had to make her comfortable as best they could on the few rugs and cloaks they possessed, whilst the ass contentedly munched the thistles that grew luxuriantly on their doorstep. And thus she was found by a priest, who threw up his hands in dismay, rushed off with his cloak bellying like a sail behind him, and suddenly burst in upon the good wife of a worthy tradesman with the astounding words: "It's a perfect disgrace that you have so many beds in your house when a saint has to lie on the floor!" In any case, Mary had a decent bed that night, but also had to resign herself to a long succession of callers.

They collected the grubby, vivacious, lazy little street-brats from the wonderful harbour, the canyon-like alleys, and the colourful market-places that lay bounded on the one side by the brilliant blue sea (so different from that of her English and Flemish youth) and with the sinister white-gleaming volcano in the background. They taught them to read, write, pray, sew, and embroider, half-ridiculed by the people for giving themselves such absurd and wholly unnecessary trouble, half gaped at as saints. The Archbishop tolerated them indulgently, albeit guardedly and distantly.

From the devout ladies who overwhelmed them during the first few days with high-flown compliments, they received, as time went on, in addition to occasional gifts of flowers and boxes of comfits, more compliments than practical assistance. Margaret Horde needs must write the most pathetic letters to the Sisters at Liége, for not one of them still possessed an undergarment that was not utterly beyond repair. Father Lee had not as much as a shirt to his back. They were living almost exclusively on the fruit that was given them or was thrown in with stray odds and ends purchased in the market, for they had not even the wherewithal to buy bread and wine, and to subsist on such a diet for any length of time was too much to expect of a healthy English stomach. And it was not even seemly that that holy poverty of theirs should cheerfully assert itself in rents and rags, as was the privilege of the brethren of the holy Arch-Mendicant, but it had to be kept strictly and modestly out of sight, so that the little community made a respectable and edi-fying impression, and incidentally managed to keep going as best it could. For the aims of the Institute were to instruct not poor children alone, but also to attract the highborn young ladies of fashionable Naples, who were taught music and Latin, the arts of writing verse and embroidery in silks, and who arrived in sumptuous litters, attended by liveried servants, at the little white house on the hill.

It was a day of rejoicing whenever the post brought them a few doubloons, though this joy was always somewhat damped by the sobering reflection that, as Mary very well knew, their feasts had, in another quarter, to be balanced by so many fasts. But it did warm your heart, this loyalty, this staunch comradeship that never questioned, never asked how much longer such a state of affairs was going to last, but simply held on, like a brave garrison during a siege.

"This is just the place for us," said Mary to her Sisters, with a wave of her hand in the direction of the sinister silhouette of Vesuvius. "I love these people who simply settle down in the shadow of that perpetual menace, taking it on trust day after day. The mountain can harm them no more than God permits, that they know—and our 'good friends' in the background cannot harm us any more, either, even if they burst in the effort."

But every time a packet of letters arrived, her heart leapt to her mouth, and she had to force herself to exchange with the courier a cheerful word or two. After which she would pace the room a couple of times, pluck a faded flower here or there from some vase, or critically examine an embroidery pattern for the sewing-class, as though for the moment that were the most important thing in the world. The Sisters, who were watching her so furtively and anxiously and who, on such occasions, would suddenly gather in her room on various pretexts, as though summoned by the bell, were not to notice how much she dreaded reading what those letters contained, and how her fingers were itching to break the seals.

For God was permitting their enemies to have things very much their own way. At Liége, matters were in a parlous state; it was only at Liége that the community itself was not entirely to be trusted. In England, one of their former associates, who had been dismissed some years before, had been writing scurrilous pamphlets purporting to be "revelations" of the internal conditions existing within the Institute. Numerous copies had found their way from one chancellery to the other, and had given rise to so much gossip and righteous indignation in devout circles that Ferdinand, the Prince Bishop, had taken it upon himself to champion the community in a solemn pastoral, threatening its aggressors with dire censure, fines and other penalties.

The autumn, however, brought a letter from the Bishop of Perugia inviting Mary to open a school in his city. Again they set out on another long trek of seventy miles along a coast still parched with summer heat, then across the Sabine Mountains into the Umbrian land, shimmering blue and violet in the soft tints of early spring. The native city of St. Francis of Assisi gave them a most impressive reception. The clergy came out to meet them in festal array, and they had to listen with what patience they could muster to a Latin Ode of sixteen verses giving a strange enough version of their life and work as it was mirrored in the poetic fancy of the Bishop's secretary. Then after a solemn *Te Deum*, three episcopal equipages carried them off to their new home, which certainly would have gladdened the heart of the Poverello himself, consisting as it did, of four bare walls, as erewhile at Naples, only this time without even doors and windows. In Italy, however, they had learnt to put up with much they would not have deemed possible in England, and even less in opulent, comfort-loving Flanders. You also learnt to submit with equanimity to ceremonial calls of six hours' duration to the accompaniment of an unending torrent of high-flown words and a veritable deluge of courtly assurances, and to bow out with the same exquisite courtesy all the good folk who stole the Lord's time with such infinite grace. Even Lennard, as Robert Wright now elected to be called (for they found a change of name a simpler matter than a change of garments), had to learn to endure these noisy, futile, and withal so charming visitors with the stolid fortitude becoming to a Christian and an Englishman.

It was too bad, though, that the violent headaches which had started at Naples and which her physician attributed to the peculiar quality of the local atmosphere, had accompanied Mary to Perugia, and, despite the wonderful breeze that came from the hills, showed no signs of abating. In addition, she had much to suffer from strange, agonizing internal pains, so that it finally became impossible to conceal them any longer from her Sisters. Soon she was barely able to write a single line without the most terrible paroxysms of pain; the slightest effort seemed to prostrate her—and their correspondence was mounting up to a truly alarming degree.

At Naples, Susan Rookwood had passed away after a short illness, and Winefrid was obliged to take over the direction of the house. In Rome, in the meantime, the Pope had died, the anxieties of the Conclave were at last over, and Cardinal Maffeo Barberini had been elected as Urban VIII. The new Pope was reputed to be a shrewd diplomat, popular with some and feared by others, was a man who lived and let live, a poet and a builder of vision, magnanimous, large-minded, most probably little interested in juristic quibblings. It might be as well to make another trip to Rome as soon as possible and sue for an audience. For the time being, however, there seemed to be little chance of obtaining one, for the changing fortunes of the German wars and troubles connected with the Mantuan succession were, no doubt, matters of graver moment to the Roman Curia than her case. One might spoil everything, too, intruding on persons at the wrong moment. Mary went first to San Cassiano to take the waters, for by now she knew that her complaint was stone. The recovery of the aged Cardinal Trescio was attributed to her prayers, and the Perugians, ever ready to worship, were already congratulating themselves, both publicly and privately, on having a new saint in their midst.

So Mary waited. What was important and what was unimportant in the sight of God? One had to see that Margaret Horde wrote a well-turned letter to her uncle on the occasion of his marriage, that a coolness that had sprung up years ago between Winefrid and a sister in England, now about to enter a convent, was brought to a satisfactory conclusion, that every House kept a well-posted letter-book. Nothing was important; everything was important; it mattered little by what name you called it.

That autumn she succeeded in obtaining an audience of the new Pope at Frascati. No one, neither friend nor enemy, was in the secret. The only thing, after all, was to place one's whole trust in the Holy Ghost and in the promptings of one's own heart. And now, perhaps, thought Mary, in the heart of the Holy Father too. He was a man as well as a sovereign. She felt a strange sense of kinship with the tall black-bearded man with the keen blue eyes—she found herself speaking more frankly and boldly than she had ever done before since her arrival in Rome. His answers were gracious, though non-committal. Even a Pope, maybe, was not always able to do as he pleased. One must wait, wait, wait.

"Go to the Pope's brother, Cardinal Barberini," said Father Lee, "he is, as you know, in the Congregation. He is a saintly Capuchin, a religious pure and simple, neither lawyer nor partisan. He will surely understand that all we seek is the greater glory of God."

In the Cardinal's little garden, laid out like that of the Capuchins at Florence where he had received the news of his election to the College of Cardinals, the audience took place on a stone bench, sunflowers and great bushes of mallows nodding over their heads.

The Cardinal stroked his long beard, obviously troubled in his mind.

"You must surely realize, Reverend Mother," he said, "that all of us, the entire Congregation, are extremely well-disposed in your regard—why, Cardinal Bandino has even been heard to say—though, in deference to your humility, I should not be repeating it here—that he would be well content to ask your blessing on his knees. We are all aware that Our Lord hath deigned to show you signal favours, and that the lives of you and your Sisters are deserving of the highest praise. But that is no reason by a long way for approving of your foundation. We see you, but we also know too many and by no means creditable things concerning your Sisters in England."

"You don't *know* them," cried Mary with some heat. "You only believe them. Why does Your Eminence prefer to believe our accusers, whom you do not know, than that which testifies in our favour and which you know to be true?"

The Capuchin shook his head. "How long is it since you were in England?" he asked.

"Six years," Mary owned sadly.

"That's it, you see: and the accusations brought against the Institute are of yesterday and to-day. After all, you are not even personally acquainted with your youngest associates; you are not even in a position to judge whether the spirit inculcated by you still lives amongst them or not—how can you know what undesirable conditions have crept in in the meantime?"

"That is not possible," said Mary with spirit. "The Superiors are still known to me—I even appointed them myself, and I'd lay my hand in the fire——"

"It does you honour, but for us it is not enough," said the Cardinal regretfully. "Believe me, we should prefer to believe what you say. You are an ardent spirit; you judge everyone by your own standard and find it impossible to conceive that any one of your number should ever fail you. We thoroughly understand your point of view, but are obliged also to take other persons' testimony into due consideration. People like you are the ones most frequently deceived."

"But I have letters," said Mary passionately, "the Holy Office is at liberty to peruse our entire correspondence—though I presume that that has already been done in part, for I know how much you distrust us. After all, I, too, am kept informed of what our Sisters are doing in England. . . ."

"You know it only in part," said the Cardinal gently. "You see, we, too, have letters and documents in our possession, written by men tried and proved, men who risk their lives daily for our holy faith, and as its confessors have languished in prisons. . . . You know, even better than we do, what it means to be a priest in England. . . . Do you mean to imply that those devout and learned men who have the good of the Church so much at heart, are all impudent traducers? You yourself would not even venture to believe any such thing. Neither could we ever believe it of you, and were you ever to assert as much, it would necessarily prejudice our confidence in you to a very considerable degree. . . ."

"Alas," cried Mary, "I verily believe that not in a hundred years were human beings ever involved in such distressful conflicts in matters wherein God alone is being sought and served. . . . You cannot understand, your Eminence, and forgive me if I say no Roman can understand how things are in England. The confusion in our midst is too great; we have no leader, and every party does and strives after what it thinks to be meet and just. Your Eminence knows yourself how stubbornly the Fathers of the Society of Jesus, which has furnished more martyrs for the Church in England, than all the other orders, opposed the restoration of the hierarchy —there was a good deal of malicious gossip at the time about our Sisters, as though they had been mixed up in it, too, when the nomination in spite of all was finally · made by Rome—and all this only because over there they call us the Jesuitesses. . . . The faithful do not dare to trust one another, for traitors and spies abound in our very midst, and persecution is responsible, not only for martyrs, but also for the worst type of apostasy— and what with all this atmosphere of secretiveness, of assumed names and false trails, playing at hide and seek, and rumours, originating one knows not whence, a great many tales may have been circulated about our

Sisters that those holy men in their solicitude for Holy Church have come to believe. . . ."

"All the same, they could not report such matters to Rome, in documents duly signed and sealed, if they had not thoroughly sifted the evidence themselves," said the Cardinal sternly.

"I know nothing of that, neither am I in a position to know," said Mary firmly; 'but I do know that my Sisters are good and do what is right in the sight of God, and I know that Heaven also blesses their efforts, and that through them much, very much, has been achieved for the glory of God and the good of His Church. Let them but show me these indictments, and I will refute them each one in turn. Your Eminence, I cannot go on like this fighting in the dark, only to be apprised by the tongue of rumour what we stand accused of. Let them give me the names of the English Sisters who have sullied our good name, let them produce dates, places, and witnesses, and I will have the matter most carefully investigated, and will exclude all from our Institute found guilty of such misdemeanour, should but a little of these indictments prove to be true. Let me see these accusations; permit me to be confronted with Mr. Rant in your presence—for that I already know, that the letters pass through him."

The Cardinal gazed at her in mild amazement. "That is not usage here," he said; "the procedure cannot be changed; it has been tried and found to be just."

Mary pressed her hands close together and was silent. She knew it was hopeless.

"We are also inclined to doubt," the Cardinal resumed, "whether a foundation of this kind, excellent though it may be in itself, is expedient at the present moment. Why should you wish just now, of all times, to harass people with problems and innovations, when in your own native-country and practically all over Europe, they are battling for the preservation and the carrying-on of our most ancient and the most sacred traditions? Is it not of greater consequence to preserve the good old things that stand in such dire peril than to embark on doubtful experiments?"

"Your Eminence, we can preserve the good old things as you call them only by venturing to try new methods. We want to keep the old faith alive in England; we want to give her religious again, and in the times in which we live, it can be done in no other way. I'm not blind, Your Eminence, I'm not self-opinionated; I quite realize that they will never understand us here in Rome—or at least not for a long, long time—also that our mode of life, to Catholic countries, may seem scandalous rather than edifying. . . . Your Eminence, I shall for the first time suggest a concession—I beg the Holy Congregation to approve the Institute only for the northern countries, only for those where it is necessary and practicable—I beg you to procure for me the authorization for England, Flanders and Germany—and, if needs be, for but one hundred religious, to enable me the more easily to watch over them, so that the Mother General may be in a position to keep each and every one of them under her supervision—and, as far as I am concerned, also that the other Orders have no longer any excuse for complaining that we steal away their candidates, though this very grievance, meseems, testifies in our favour: for, were not the call for such a life in many hearts, our efforts alone could not possibly bring us such an influx."

"Venture," said the Cardinal. "You are extremely fond of that word. We are not."

"No," said Mary softly, "and yet on venturing

depends to-day and for aye the future of the Kingdom of God."

She could not fathom the meaning of the strange look the Cardinal bent on her.

"May Our Lord give you strength to seek His holy will in all things," was all he said. Then, painfully, he rose from his seat, blessed the woman kneeling humbly at his feet, and left her almost hurriedly, still shaking his head.

The following morning, Mary received a letter from the Congregation of Cardinals informing her that the matter in hand was already settled: His Holiness would on no account confirm the Institute. The Italian schools would have to be closed down.

"Now the battle is beginning," said Mary with pale cheeks but flashing eyes to Barbara Babthorpe. She wrote to the most influential relative of Paul V, Cardinal Borgia, the idol of the people, and he was successful in procuring a postponement. No final decision was arrived at; war had broken out in the Valtalline and the plague was bearing down on Sicily. Mary found fresh supporters. Fathers Suarez and Lessius, both noted theologians, wrote long treatises about her Institute, pointing out that it in no way contravened the precepts of Holy Church, but, on the contrary, even supplied a long-felt need.

Oh, Mary did all that was within her power to do. She had the treatises copied and sent them to the Cardinals of the Congregation, though what she did was without any hope of success. She knew that the fate that had long been hanging over her, like the threatening shadow of Vesuvius over the city of Naples, was now slowly and relentlessly bearing down upon her. Every day in some different church she attended the Forty Hours Prayer; to

L

her it was a marvellous consolation to behold her Lord in
the Blessed Sacrament shining like some changeless star
in the darkness of her night. And that light grew ever
clearer, the more the darkness closed in upon her. All
that she prayed for now was the courage to persevere
along a path of which the end was not even in sight.
She was not greatly surprised, though nobody understood her enigmatic smile and the meaning way in which
she nodded her head when, soon after, the Bull of Suppression was finally promulgated. A noisy demonstra-
tion of the pupils and their mothers before the palaces of
the Vicar General and Donna Constanza Barberini did
not change the course of events. The Sisters packed their
bundles and left the Holy City. In the church of San
Marco, Mary knelt once more before the gleaming
mystery of the monstrance, and in her heart she heard
the words: "Can you drink the chalice that I shall drink?"

"Aye, Lord," she said simply, "I'm not nearly tired
yet."

On the long journey to Naples, she spoke hardly a
word. But when she sat at table, the Sisters, depressed
and silent around her, whilst a wild, almost angry sunset
slowly faded over the harbour, bathing in its sinister
glory the empty, silent house, with the joyous sound
of children's voices stilled, she gazed round at her little
circle with a swift bright smile, and all held their breath,
for the face they saw before them had long been to them
a stranger.

"Why do you all gaze at me so dismally?" she said
and laughed. "Are we not still the merry companions
as of old, who sixteen years ago at Hungerford House
pledged ourselves to the great game? Win, Jane, Meg,
you others, surely you remember? Of course, we've
grown old with the passage of time, and it was only

just this moment I realized that we had—but we're not so old but that we cannot seek work somewhere else and find it, seeing that they've so unkindly thrown us out here. I shall give you three days to pack and to pay farewell visits, and then we'll move on to Germany. There's still room for us there."

*   *   *   *   *

Thus we now find them embarked on another journey, Mary and Mary Poyntz, Elizabeth Cotton and little Hester, and, of course, Father Lee, likewise grown grey in years of faithful service, and Lennard Morris. It was St. Martin's Day. An icy blast blew from the Alps, but they dared not put off their departure, for they wanted to reach Munich before Tilly and his opponents, the Brunswick and Danish troops, moved to southern Germany. Graubundten and Veltlin were aflame with revolt; every pass and even the plain of Lombardy were swarming with Savoyard, French, German, Swiss and Papal soldiery. The northern Italian courts, all connected in some way by marriage with Austria and Spain, and where, at least among the ladies, a letter from Father Domenico di Gesù Maria was received with the same implicit faith as the Holy Gospel itself, flung open their gates to the travellers who brought with them letters of introduction from so saintly a man. Florence, Parma, Castello Castiglione near Siena vied with one another in their lavish hospitality and commiserated with the pilgrims who were so determined to venture into Europe's storm-centre, the hapless German Empire, so long ravaged by fire and sword.

It was a terrible journey over the wintry Lake of Como, across the Great St. Bernard, through the snowed-up

pass, through heavy drifts and icy blasts, doubly keen
and searching after the years they had spent in Italy. To
add to their troubles, their money ran out, and the people
of Graubundten, hostile to Catholics, often denied them
as much as a bite of food or a night's lodging. Finally
they reached the Tyrol. There they began to wish that
they, or at least some of their number, knew a little
German. Every now and then, you seemed to catch a
word or a phrase that vaguely reminded you of the
dialect you had heard years ago in Flanders—the little
Mary had managed to pick up during a stay in Cologne
had grown rusty for lack of use—but this German at any
rate seemed totally different.

On Christmas Eve they reached Feldkirch. The stars
hung over the snow-covered mountains. The snow lay
thick on the roofs and along the streets, and down in the
valley bobbed yellow specks of light from the lanterns
carried by the faithful trudging to midnight mass in the
parish church.

"It's just five years since we arrived in Rome," said
Mary. "Who would have thought . . ." No, one
mustn't think back, nor wonder why. God alone knew
why it had to be thus. It was nice to be once more in a
Catholic country, which, in its turn, was so very different from the south, where they had never felt really
at home.

The parish church was dark and full of mysterious
corners, but the candles were beginning to gleam, and
a large Crib, all complete with sheep and shepherds,
had been set up in the foreground. Never had the pilgrims seen anything like it before. A warm smell of the
stables rose from the worshippers and from the shaggy
sheepskin coats of the men who knelt before it. The
recital of the rosary began, with a kind of droning hearti-

ness, strangely soothing in its only half comprehended
rhythm, like the murmur of a great mountain stream.
Then the boys from the Jesuit College began to sing like
angels, and for an hour it was just home, that home that
is the Holy Catholic Church.

Mass was long over; in the big square before the
church, dense crowds of people slowly dispersed in
long straggling streams of light, trickling away through
dim portals or dipping down into the depths of the
valley beneath a soaring green-blue Christmas sky,
bright with gigantic stars. By the Crib a few candles
were still burning, slowly guttering out in great waxen
tears, and every now and then you could hear their heavy
drip-drip in a silence growing ever chiller. The stranger
Sisters kneeling in the bench before the Crib shivered in
utter weariness, but where were they to go? Where after
midnight were they like to find accommodation? Lennard had fallen asleep where he knelt, and his young
face, haggard with hunger and fatigue, framed with the
straw-coloured hair that hung down over his unshaven
cheeks, might have been that of one of the carved shepherds clustering around the Holy Child.

Mary suddenly became aware that somebody was
tugging at her sleeve. It was Mistress Cecily Griesmaicrin,
the parish priest's sister, who had picked out the unknown
religious already at the first Kyrie eleison, and much to
her distraction in prayer, had been racking her brains
about them ever since, and now in a reverent whisper
sought to appease her consuming curiosity as to where
they had come from and whither they were bound. It
was not much that she was able to glean from their
replies, but she did manage to gather that they had
come from Rome and had no place to lay their heads.
And just at that very moment, Lennard opened his eyes,

good, hungry, dog-tired eyes, like those of a little child, and for the good lady that was quite enough. With her two sturdy arms she dragged the strangers up to their feet so that their threadbare old cloaks nearly gave beneath the strain.

"Now you've got to come straight along with me and have a decent meal: we've got beds, too, in plenty. . . ."

She groped her way out before them, clutching the blue cowl she wore over her head tight to her bony apple-red cheeks, for the night-wind swept keenly down from the regions of eternal ice. Then, with her little lantern dancing and twinkling comfortably before them, they followed her as though in a dream.

It was only in the big living-room of the presbytery, where the dishes amongst the fir-green on the white-spread table steamed and exuded a most delectable fragrance, and the brown-timbered ceiling spreading above the low room like a benediction, glowed a warm gold in the candlelight, that the Sisters noticed for the first time that Mary was not in their midst. Mistress Cecily hustled her guests who were standing about, still benumbed with cold, towards the bench in the ingle-nook, whilst the parish priest manfully embarked on a conversation in a weird and wonderful Latin with Father Lee, whose own Latin, in its turn laboured under the handicap of a strong English accent, interspersed with an occasional smattering of Italian.

Before the Crib a solitary candle was still burning, and the foreign lady was still kneeling there, with her arms outstretched, so that her shadow, like that of a giant in flight, spread over communion rails and altar steps, and, even from the threshold, Mistress Cecily could hear her groaning aloud like one in sore pain. As she crept closer, softly and fearfully, she saw that the pale face, set to the semblance of a mask, was bathed in tears, and that the eyes were wide open and terrible, eyes such as one sees only in a dying face. It was then that the stout-hearted old lady, who also knew something of transcendental things, realized that here something was going forward that was not meant for other eyes to see. Quietly she laid the key beside the kneeling woman, who was not even conscious of her presence, then hurriedly groped her way out again, carefully leaving the door ajar.

It was only when the guests at the presbytery had long appeased the pangs of hunger and were sitting in a comfortable glow before their empty plates—Lennard alone still munching away blissfully with bulging cheeks, for a regular meal with meat and beer had not fallen to his lot for many months past—whilst the great green-tiled stove exuded a gentle heat in waves of pleasant drowsiness, that Mary made her appearance, and not even then, was she able to muster up a smile.

In the darkness of the guest-chamber, submerged in the unwonted luxury of enormous feather beds, Mary Poyntz, in whom fear had cast out sleep, finally ventured to put the timid question she was burning to ask, only to receive the reply: "I was praying for the conversion of England, and much was revealed to me of which I find it impossible to speak."

And in the dim, blue-green snow-light that filtered in through the windows, Mary, not daring to move, saw that for long after that their Mother still sat erect in her bed, and later she heard a sound of stifled sobbing, so bitter and despairing that it seemed to her that never had she heard its like before nor in that indomitable woman have ever deemed possible.

On the following morning, whilst they were following

Mistress Cecily up the long flight of wooden steps that led to the little Capuchin church, where the people were already assembling for High Mass, Mary, her face still ravaged with the traces of her sleepless night, said to her Sisters, like one who speaks in a dream: "Pray, I beg you, to-day for our poor King Charles."

"Is His Majesty then threatened with some danger?" inquired little Hester anxiously, whilst the others gazed at one another in startled bewilderment. Mary, however, quickly averted her face, so that her companions could only hear the tears in her voice: "My Sisters, if I knew that Our Lord loved me with such a love as He manifests towards that unhappy royal soul, I should die of very joy.... Oh, it is a terrible mystery that in respect to the grace of God we are free to do what we will!"

By noon, the news had spread like wildfire amongst all the devout matrons and maidens who came to the presbytery to proffer their Christmas greetings or to partake of a draught of something hot after their long tramp to church, that its hospitable roof sheltered one who had come straight from Rome and had seen the Holy Father; also that Mistress Griesmaierin, were she but at liberty to speak, could say a good deal, only that she knew what was right and proper.... And that afternoon, Mary suddenly found herself the storm-centre of half the parish, besieged by mothers and their daughters, whilst the men, and even a few lads, stood about awkwardly in the doorway, removed their hats as though they were in church, and shuffled away again, devoutly muttering to themselves. The women talked at her in their inarticulate ponderous way, some with tears in their eyes, some shouting as though she were deaf, since she obviously did not understand a single word of what they were saying; others pressed her hands with their toil-

worn fingers, left, almost shamefacedly, parcels of good
nourishing food on the table beside her, and crossed
themselves frequently and fervently. Mary understood
but one thing, for she could read the hidden secrets of
the soul, and that was that there was much silent heart-
ache in their eyes and in the compressed hardness of their
lips. She only said again and again: "I will pray for you,
and do you pray for me," nodding encouragingly to one
and all. But the people who elbowed and jostled one
another on the stairs and in the long passage below, already
trampled full of snow and mud, asked everyone who
emerged from the room: "What did she say then?"
and really did not seem to be aware that they had received
no answer whatever to their question, for the faces of
those that passed them were as radiant as though they
had just seen the Three Wise Men in the flesh before
their very eyes and had received the freedom of the
kingdom of heaven. And those who had still to wait
patiently wrapped their *loden* cloaks more closely
around them and stood there like blocks of wood for
another long hour. And after it was all over, they in
their turn opined that it had all been very much worth
waiting for.

There were others, too, that came—bearded Capuchins,
Jesuit professors, Cistercians from Mehrerau, and Friar
Preachers, who happened to be at Feldkirch for the Feast,
and they, too, asked her all manner of strange questions
about the outcome of the war, one even about the end
of the world, and much about spiritual matters, too.
They went away silently, even looking a little abashed
and you wondered why. But there were also others
who departed with faces like children who had unex-
pectedly found their Christmas stocking filled to over-

flowing, when all they had counted on was a poor penny piece. Mary, however, was half-dead with fatigue and utterly at a loss to explain what the whole procession was all about. Silently she ate a few spoonfuls of food and finally fell asleep like some weary warrior after the fray.

The following morning, they were sent in a conveyance to Innsbruck, rigged out with new *loden* mantles and, thanks to the motherly care of Mistress Cecily, with their travelling bags filled to bursting with luscious Tyrolean ham and crisp round loaves, Christmas cake, apples, and other things both useful or good to eat. From the snow-covered steps, crimson in the light of dawn, the parish priest and his sister waved until they were out of sight, and it was Easter before any visitor to the presbytery could hope to get away without hearing the full story of their wonderful Pilgrim.

Mary, however, resumed her journey, with some delay, to be sure, but with her heart full of the sweetness of Christmas consolation and peace. Their road now went eastwards, past the Hospice on the Arlberg, through villages deep in snow, where giant bright-coloured St. Christophers looked down from church walls into the valley below, across the Trisanna, which tumbled boiling and foaming from green blocks of ice, then on along the Inn past castle-crowned summits.

At the new castle at Innsbruck, there were again letters to be presented from Father Domenico, letters that opened not only the doors, but also the hearts of Archduke Leopold and his lovely Medici Duchess. The pilgrims visited the Jesuit Fathers in the Sillgasse, bringing greetings from the College in Rome, were delighted and amazed to discover their own King Arthur among the "Bronze Men" guarding the Emperor's tomb in the Court Church, and when they stepped out of its solemn twilight, glimmering with the Christmas decorations, yet another surprise awaited them, for the veil of mist that had hung over the town was now rent in twain, and a great chain of mountains dazzled their wondering eyes, looming in snow-white majesty against the background of a bright blue sky.

One of the Archduke's coaches took them on to Hall, where the Canonesses from their windows, blazoned with armorial bearings, shook their heads dubiously at the unfamiliar habits, whilst the children ran after the court equipage singing:

> "Und die schöne Claudia,
> tipfel, tipfel, tipfel,
> Domine exaudia . . ."

Then, slowly and in piercing cold weather, the journey was continued by water. A burgher's daughter of Hall, who had succumbed to the spell of the foreign ladies, now travelled with them. Anna Maria Grunwald was her name, and for them it was a good thing at last to have a capable interpreter amongst their number. The good Sisters at the convent had taught her something of sick-nursing, how to apply poultices and prepare draughts, so Mary Poyntz arranged, thus causing a hint of jealous feeling amongst the older Sisters, that Anna was to attend to their Mother's needs, for the bouts of pain and the attacks of sickness had again become so violent that they were barely able to travel as much as twelve miles a day. Nevertheless, she was the prey of a feverish restlessness they had never known in her before, and which her more intimate companions regarded as a dangerous symptom. They noticed, too, how, despite her pitiful weakness, their Mother spent more and more time in prayer, that she sought to be alone and avoided converse with them, and, for the first time since they had known her, her eyes seemed to meet theirs like those of a stranger. She no longer inquired after little Hester's chilblains or Elizabeth Cotton's cough, no longer when they halted for a rest, did she insist on a personal examination of Mary Poyntz's shoes and her poor sore feet, forgot to ask Father Lee about his breviary and Lennard after his appetite—and it was only then that they realized how accustomed they had grown to all these constant innumerable tokens of her motherly love. The Mother General, they told themselves, must be very sick indeed, or the Lord was revealing to her some very strange things in prayer.

On the Feast of St. Thomas of Canterbury, they were sitting together in the swiftly falling dusk around the stove in their inn—from Wasserburg they were moving on by coach—and Father Lee after some brief devotions in honour of the martyr of the English Church, was reading the ever-consoling Gospel of the day: "I am the Good Shepherd; and I know mine and mine know me. As the Father knoweth me, and as I know the Father; and I lay down my life for my sheep. And other sheep I have that are not of this fold: them also must I bring, and they shall hear my voice, and there shall be one fold and one shepherd."

Very dim burnt the lamp in the shadow of the great stove. The air was stuffy with the smell of oil and smoke and fried fat. Outside the snow fell unceasingly in fine flakes that were steadily mounting up against the window-panes.

"Anna Maria," said Mary suddenly, "what is Munich?"

"That's the place whither we are bound, and where the Lord Elector lives."

"And tell me, what is the *Anger?* Are there not religious there, and are they not called after St. James?"

"God bless my soul!" cried Anna, crossing herself in her alarm, "it's all as true as true can be, but Reverend Mother could not possibly know it for all that."

"Anna Maria," said Mary, so softly that the others could not catch her words, "both you and I shall go there. I shall be taken there as a false prophetess, and you will become a nun in the Convent."

The days were gradually getting longer, and there was a touch of spring in the air. The Isar was no longer blocked with drift-ice, nor dark and turbulent with melted snow from the mountains. On some days, it even reflected an Easter-blue sky, and though its banks were not yet bright with flowers, they were gay on Sundays with people decked out in their best, anxious to make the most of the sunshine. For the winter had been loth to die and had lingered so long that it seemed difficult to recall what a green meadow or a blossoming bush had once looked like, and you remembered last year's summer much as you did your own childhood—you knew that it had really been and that others would go through the same experience again, but as far as you were concerned, it had gone for ever.

"Yes, spring's on the way," said Mary to her secretary, Elizabeth Cotton, for Mother Mary Poyntz was now Superior of the new Paradeiser House at Munich and had both hands about as full as she could manage. "Strange how the world has changed, isn't it, Elizabeth? It seems almost like a dream, when you think back on Christmas—do you remember that terrible journey across the mountains? God occasionally puts our willingness to the test, to see whether the readiness we protested was only lip-service or whether He might take us at our word. . . . When we crossed the Alps it was almost as fugitives and exiles who had no place whereon to lay their heads; to-day we scarcely know how we are to cope with all this marvellous work. Just write again to Liége and tell them to send me three more Sisters."

Musingly Mother Elizabeth cut a fresh quill. Nobody would ever have thought either that the Mother General was going to make such a good recovery; that in itself was little short of a miracle. She had not looked so young and vigorous for years, thought Elizabeth, gazing at her shyly, her heart throbbing with the same love and devotion as in the early days of her novitiate. Tall and very erect, she sat there in her armchair, the sober black of the veil and habit setting off the clear fresh colouring of the face framed by the narrow linen collar and the white bandeau. A lovely picture she made, indeed; but when you looked into her eyes you forgot all the rest, those wonderful dark eyes, despite their depth as clear as a flame, looking straight into your heart, so that you almost shrank from them and yet could not avert your own; those eyes that knew all there was to know about you and yet betrayed nothing, that were so warm and friendly, and yet so full of reverence and remoteness, no matter whether she spoke to a child or a novice, to the Lord Elector or to a distinguished prelate.

She had also, thank God, learned to laugh again, that warm, deep-throated laugh of hers, which reminded you somehow of the way our Lennard laughed—but if you had known her, as we of the old guard did, you'd have to own, all the same, that in those other days, before the Italian years, her mouth was very different, full and tender, where now there was just a line, clear-cut and firm, but hard, too—sometimes even uncomfortably hard.

"You're dreaming instead of writing," said Mary patiently; "I even suspect that the spring has gone to your head like new wine. Wake up, my dear, we have no time to lose. The Lord Elector presented us with this fine house to do some good hard work in it. Our little German girls are so bright and so industrious, that teaching them is a real pleasure. This is work very different from the kind we had in Rome, eh? Ah, if only I had the necessary teachers—ten, twenty more. For the work I could give them to do, even two hundred would not be too many."

Her fingers drummed softly on the arms of her chair, and her mouth hardened again. Ah, as far as numbers went, there was staff and to spare at Liége, Cologne and Trèves, only you could not turn them to any real account. What, she wondered, was the reason. To her it was one of the most tragic riddles of all that a soul could be called to that holy and noble vocation, to that new way revealed to her by her Lord for His greater glory, only then somehow to fall short of its sublime destiny, to lapse into indolence, luke-warmness, and, worst thing of all, cowardice. What might be the reason? They began by braving the opposition of their parents and the penal laws, became voluntary exiles from their native-country, staked all they possessed boldly and generously on the great venture—and then, suddenly, maybe after many years, some chance rumour, some idle gossip, an adverse opinion expressed by some Father, sufficed to make them throw up everything, in weary acquiescence to lay down their arms—or even to abandon the religious life, and later on to break the bright courage of others with their old-womanish niggling, to swell the perpetual hum of gossip that buzzed around the Institute like a swarm of poisonous insects, almost hiding it even from its friends...

The windows overlooking the Weinstrasse were open, and the sound of the school-bell clanged through the house. It was followed by a tremendous rustle and bustle on the lower floor, as of books and stiff petticoats, then the whole young swarm burst through the gate. From her window, Mary looked down on them below, where they were standing about, racing, putting their heads together, little white and coloured caps and ruffs, thick and thin plaits and mops of curls. Over there a couple of them were dawdling near the steps, lying in wait for Mother Mary Poyntz. No sooner did she appear than they made a rush at her to bob a curtsey and kiss her hands.

Oh, those girlish hearts, tempestuous, defenceless, fond, tender, worshipping hearts! What lovelier task than to serve them, watch over them, cherish, guide, and instruct them? Her own heart swelled high with a warm happiness and, at the same time, with a great, dark sadness. What in the world could it be, she mused, that made their life strike others as outrageous and extravagant, that stirred up so much suspicion, so much hatred against them? She understood it less and less. Her way was new —or rather, it had once been new, for eighteen years is a long time. When we began, our youngest novices of to-day were not even born. . . . Was that not a long enough test to prove one's worth in the sight of God and man? Surely they had demonstrated that the life and the work were well adapted to many different types of women of many different countries, both for themselves and for others. What was there in them to-day that could be called dangerous or adventurous? Provided they were left in peace, was it not the most natural and inoffensive thing in the world, their sisterly life in community, their schools, and their life with their children? Were not all

the parents both grateful and well content? Were not
the girls themselves advancing in wisdom and grace
before God and man? Did not each one of the Sisters
feel in her heart of hearts that God's blessing rested on
her work?

Why, then, all this inveterate hostility?

"Are you aware, Mother Elizabeth, that our good
friends, the 'Jerusalems'"—thus the English Ladies had
dubbed their enemies, because they helped them to merit
the heavenly Jerusalem—"have already brought themselves to the notice of our Elector? He has received a
nice long letter in which all the old stories are dished up
again with which we have been served time after time
—did he know what kind of people he had let loose on
his beautiful city; did he likewise know that we were up
to our ears in debt and should most certainly abuse his
kindness to serve our own ends?"

"And what did His Highness say?" asked Elizabeth
tremulously. It was too bad; hardly were they beginning
to enjoy this unwonted feeling of security than trouble
seemed to be brewing all over again.

Mary laughed long and heartily. "Our Elector is
really a man in a thousand. What did he say? 'The
devil's behind this,' is what he said, 'so we'll give him
one over the snout just to show him what we think of
him here in Bavaria.' And his answer to the letter was
to fix our endowment at two thousand gulden instead of
fifteen hundred, as he had originally intended. Child,
if we had had all that money at Perugia!"

Mother Elizabeth breathed a deep sigh of relief.

"He even sent me the fatal letter," Mary continued.
"To be sure, I was not permitted to read it myself, but
the Dean of Our Lady's Church read it to me. All the

M

same I have a pretty shrewd suspicion as to who was the author. Who it was, my dear child? That you don't need to know. It is quite sufficient for us to discuss our enemies with Our Lord and not with our fellow-men, and you can include him in your Memento without mentioning him by name."

One evening, the senior Sisters were assembled in high council, Father Lee also being present.

"We've had a good mail to-day," Mary announced. "Winefrid writes from Naples that the novitiate is flourishing—I'm almost inclined to think that it's a blessing rather than otherwise that they no longer have a school—and that they have twelve new postulants, all ladies from Catania. Also there is a request from Sicily, asking us to make a foundation there. That, however, will not be such an easy matter, because of the Decree. But it does show that our Institute in Italy is again in better odour—it will soon be high time for us to present another petition to Rome."

Father Lee fidgeted slightly in his seat.

"But there's something else, even more important. We are to found a house in Vienna. His Majesty, the Emperor Ferdinand, has most graciously placed at our disposal a building to serve as convent and school. Our Elector had told him about our work here, and their Majesties think that we might prove useful allies in the unceasing war they are waging against heresy. Now what think you of it?"

By way of a prelude to what he had to say, Father Lee unfolded with some ceremony a sheet of paper that he had been crumpling nervously in his hands.

"Father Gerard has written me," he said. "He thinks we should proceed warily in regard to new foundations, organizing one model house well and thoroughly rather than straining and striving to erect others—even though they were offered us by the Emperor himself," he concluded with a certain stern emphasis.

"He's heard that from his Fathers in Vienna," said Mary indulgently; "and that, after all, is nothing in the nature of a Divine revelation."

But Father Lee still looked serious, reiterating, "By the good it does, a single well-run house has the advantage over many houses launched with a small and inadequate staff. Therefore it is better for us to confine ourselves to comparatively few foundations and to carry on those we have undertaken properly, so that others can see what might be achieved, and would be achieved, if only we had the necessary workers. And those workers once they were approved, would most certainly be forthcoming from the best blood of every country, also from our own. . . ."

Mother Win Bedingfield was of the same opinion. As it was, the Munich foundation had deprived the Cologne community of its best forces. At Liége, things had been at sixes and sevens ever since Winefrid had been called away to take over the Naples house. At Trèves, too, they were beginning to realize that it was not advisable for young and untried religious to be entrusted with responsible positions soon after concluding their novitiate.

"Barbara Babthorpe was twenty years old when I appointed her Superior at St. Omer," said Mary with great decision. "Not one of us was any older when we began the work, and, God knows, it was more difficult then than it is now. I don't know why we've grown so timorous and cautious these days."

"The times were different," said Win Bedingfield;

"the times of the early Christians were also different from those of to-day."

"And the people were different, too," said Father Lee gently. For the space of a brief moment the eyes of the old comrades met in a bright joyous glance full of old memories.

"We are no longer able to do what they did, Mother General," said Win humbly, "the first are the first—in every Order it hath been thus."

"All the same, the house in Vienna is going to be started," said Mary calmly. "We cannot possibly reject the Emperor's offer, it would prove too prejudicial for the future of our cause. After that, we will ponder well our Father's good counsels and be both prudent and cautious."

She gave Father Lee a bright smile, and he realized that as far as he was concerned the game was up. A marvellous and a saintly woman, but obstinate as a mule.

Then, suddenly, he became aware that he was again being called to account:"And why did Father Gerard write that to you and not to me?"

"Hm—I suppose people still have their prejudices. He sends you greetings and thought you might be writing to your brother at the novitiate of Ghent, then he would be able to read your letters too."

Mary burst into a hearty laugh. "Be guileful as the serpent, eh? And then they abuse us poor women for our craftiness and treachery!—No, your Reverence, I fight with other weapons.—Elizabeth, just draft a letter to Naples: Mother Win is to be Superior, Mother Jane Brown to take over the novices in her stead, and Margaret Genison is the Superior of my choice for Vienna."

*   *   *   *   *

In June, she set out for the Austrian Dominions, and this time her journey was very different from all the others. "We're getting above ourselves," growled Lennard, when the court equipages rolled up that were to take them on to Passau. To Linz they proceeded by way of the Danube. It was wonderful, drifting slowly down the great river, dark forests and towering rocks on either side alternating with endless strips of brush, lush green and studded with low shrubs, whilst the trees along the banks still bristled with the shaggy loam deposit left behind by the spring floods. Our Lady's sanctuaries looked down on them from the summits of gently rising hills; the Pöstlingberg loomed ahead with its little white church, at Grein there was the dangerous whirlpool to be negotiated, through a wilderness of jagged rocks—then before them rose the mighty monastery of Melk, majestic, imperious, glittering in the sun from its rock above the green river. In the steep little fields climbing up the banks, patches of scarlet poppies glowed amidst the whitish gold of ripening corn; the perfume of roses was wafted over the rippling water from the gardens of high-perched castles; ancient crevassed walls dozed amidst wooded heights; goats browsed amongst the crumbling rocks, with the steep terraces of green vineyards twining their way in between—a world enchanted and remote.

Sometimes they passed boats rowing upstream that hardly seemed to move against the strong current: and there was something strangely exotic in the haunting melody the men from Hungary sang on their heavily laden decks. Rafts drifted swiftly downstream whilst here and there, some lone ferry plied to and fro between white, steep-walled market towns. Then they passed Krems, where the Jesuit Fathers were engaged in mission work in the Emperor's name, in an effort to win the still covertly Lutheran district back to the faith.

Mary gazed back at the vanishing towers. Much that had been said on the boat had not escaped her. Alas, what an impenetrable mystery it was that God's cause was served with such strange instruments. Great was the young Emperor's zeal, and God bless him for it. It was also his undoubted right and his duty as a Christian sovereign to purge his dominions of heresy and exact submission to Holy Church. . . . But Mary had not forgotten the unspeakable misery and oppression of her own childhood, how were it possible, indeed? Here, too, other men and women were suffering in the same way,—for their false tenets, to be sure, but homeland was homeland, and exile was exile, and disgrace and imprisonment and recusant fines had the same bitterness everywhere, for the hearts of men were the same, whether Catholic or heretic. God have pity on us all!

Then Klosterneuburg, with its high roofs and soaring towers, also lay behind them in the exquisite silky luminosity of the sunset air. Here the colouring was much softer, more melancholy and subdued. Mary turned towards the stern deck; obliquely from the water, high on the left, rose a steep mountain crowned with a castle, that hung over the river with the menace of a clenched fist. Behind it, the summery green of beech forests stretched away over long ridges of hills. On the other bank, however, the land lay as flat as the palm of your hand, brown with marshy reeds. Endlessly the plain rolled on to the east, until your gaze was lost in a shimmering distance, from which came a hot breath, heavy and exotic. A strange spasmodic tremor passed through Mary's frame, and she beckoned her cousin and serving-man who, like herself, was lost in his own silent dreams, as he gazed down at the water.

"Down this river," she said, "our ancestors once passed on their way to the Holy Sepulchre with Richard the Lionhearted—your ancestors and mine, Robbie. Strange that I should think of it just now!"

Once more they found themselves in a strange house, in an unknown city, surrounded by strange faces. The house was known as *Stoss im Himmel* and was a large building, practically new. Eighteen families had had to move out at the Emperor's orders to make room for the new religious; it had been the talk of the town and there were some who were not any too pleased about it. But, of course, as everyone knew, the Emperor would willingly vacate his own royal palace at the Burg to make room for monks or nuns, and he would be more likely to pledge his loyal city of Vienna than to abandon the idea of such a foundation. The entire court, too, had to wait three whole days for the annual summer removal to Prague, because their Majesties insisted on attending the consecration of the house in person; and, when all was said and done, there was nothing much worth seeing at that—a few elderly ladies in shabby black garments, and stiffly starched collars and caps, very much like ordinary burghers' widows, together with a grey-haired clergyman—and that was all. Whatever they did, you might be sure, wouldn't be up to much. It was not likely that they were going to succeed where others had failed, and that they were going to drag the cart out of the mud in which dear old Vienna had been firmly stuck for this many a year. If any were likely to do so, it was surely the Jesuit Fathers with their beautiful sermons and their learned professors, not to mention their famous confessors, who were always playing Divine

Providence a bit, especially at court. One of them, too, was Confessor to their Majesties, Father Lamormain. Now, the old Carmelite had been a man of a different stamp, the one, you know, who sent the Bohemians packing to the devil at the White Mountain . . . but the Holy Father in Rome had refused to let him go, so, in such a case, even our Emperor had been obliged to give in. Maybe it was Father Lamormain who had brought in these Englishwomen? He was a foreigner himself. As if the Lord Bishop Khlesl hadn't done more than enough already for pious women. Why, it was only five years ago that he presented the nuns of St. Nicholas in the Singerstrasse with the house of the Poor Clares, who had moved to Pressburg, in order to enable them to open a girls' school. He had renewed the endowment of the Sisters of St. Jerome in order to provide a home and schooling for twenty orphans of the city. He had heavily subsidized the Augustine nuns in the Himmelpfortgasse so that they were able to rebuild and enlarge the old convent; children were to be received in their enclosure and brought up in those principles of virtue and piety as are only to be acquired behind convent walls. So the Englishwomen might just as well have stayed where they were—only, of course, it was said that the order had as its secret designation "Mothers of the Society of Jesus," and that explained a lot. It was not supposed to be talked about, of course, but we shall see what we shall see.

The *Stoss im Himmel* was provided with an impressive new entrance, with a plaster sunburst surrounding the sacred monogram IHS over the gateway. Funds were forthcoming, the Emperor contributing six hundred gulden a year and the Empress four hundred. The community had no chapel of their own, but neither had they had one at the Paradeiser Haus, where the Sisters used to say their prayers at Our Lady of the Crypt. In Vienna, their nearest church, Maria Stiegen, was just round the corner. It was a poor little church, not to be compared with the imposing Jesuit church *am Hof*, or with their other new church in the Bäckerstrasse, still in course of construction, next door to the University, which for the last few years had been once more under the direction of the Fathers. Maria Stiegen looked as though it were hiding itself away from the big churches of the Scottish Benedictines and of the Augustines, not to mention St. Stephen's. But the Sisters soon decided that theirs was the loveliest church in all Vienna. None had such an exquisitely graceful bee-hive cupola to crown its tower, like a flower-cup fashioned of interlacing tendrils and long prickly thorns, so that sunset and sunrise gleamed through it like the purple through the arches of the Imperial crown. In no church of Vienna was there such a dim mysterious atmosphere, fragrant with the incense of generations of prayer; none had such deep portals beneath stone canopies springing like some delicate growth from a background of bluish rock. None had within such a mighty solitary Gothic arch between nave and altar, soaring, as it were, from an unending stream of devotion, so that you instinctively folded your hands in prayer when you gazed at it. And of nights, if you could not sleep, you heard the mighty Danube rushing down below by the Fischerstiege, where the Passau boats lie, so that you could almost imagine the little church standing like a lighthouse watching over the open sea. It was a holy place, as anyone could feel, once he had prayed there, an unfailing source of hidden favours and renewed hope for those who still sought it out.

And the new school in the shadow of Maria Stiegen

flourished in its turn. By the autumn, its Superior, Helen Clifford, was able to enter the four hundredth name on the school roll, day-girls all, though there were also four boarders from castles in the great northern forest and on the Thaya. The Fathers in the Bäckerstrasse had been kind and neighbourly, and were soon extolling the girls' beautiful Latin exercise-books and their excellent singing in church, even though they still gave pride of place to their own boys' choir, but that, of course, was because of the voices, not the musical direction. The Empress sent her ladies-in-waiting to the needlework classes and had the beautiful designs sent to the Palace for her inspection. All was going well, Mary assured herself. The girls were certainly not learning more than was necessary. If only the mothers of the last genera-tion had been better instructed in religion and virtue, so many of their men-folk would certainly not have lapsed from their holy faith. Above all, the girls were to acquire a thorough knowledge of Latin, so that they should be able to follow the offices of Holy Church and explain them to their own children and the other members of their household, otherwise piety was only too apt to degenerate into superstition, routine, or scrupulousness. What time remained was to be devoted to a study of the language of the Church, needlework for the altar alone to have precedence. The Fathers had said that learning for women stimulated pride and was harmful to virtue. They need have no anxiety on that score; learn-ing must and would become so general in their com-munity that there should be no grounds for such com-plaint. All this she had so much at heart that Mother Elizabeth had to send her the best exercise-books from Munich, and despite all her other work, she insisted on going through every one of them herself, so as to be able to encourage the best pupils with words of praise and coloured images. "I fear these subtle wenches have some help at home to make their themes," she wrote to Mary Poyntz, "but you will look to them for that!"

In the autumn came yet another dangerous and flattering commission: would she open a house at Pressburg? Cardinal Pazmany, the moving spirit in the Catholic regeneration of Hungary, had heard of her work; it was something after his own heart, for his methods were less rigorous than those of his Imperial lord. Why, indeed, should the refractory be forced into submission by outlawry, excommunication, taxation and dragoons? Such things only embittered people and engendered a secret hatred all the more dangerous for being secret. The old faith should be restored to the people in the arms of mothers, in cradle-songs, in children's play, and the festivals of youth; wives and sweethearts were the ones to implant it firmly in every heart; an objective like that of the new Institute was a God-given instrument for achieving what the Cardinal had in mind.

Mary's mind was torn by bitter conflicts. By way of precaution, Father Lee had given her a letter from their oldest and most faithful friend to accompany her on her journey. "It is contrary to every dictate of prudence to proceed thus," he wrote urgently, imploringly. But it was surely contrary to the love of God and man to hesitate when a gate like this was opened before one—the gate to a whole land!

"God preserve me from a prudence that is directly opposed to charity!" Oh, how hard, how cruelly hard it was, not to have the right people for so vast a field of work and so abundant a harvest as was waiting for them everywhere. . . . Winefrid would again have to send her more recruits. She must needs find more novices, say twenty, by the end of the year; she would have to see where she was going to get them. All this, to be sure, would exact a heavy toll on the health and strength of the older Sisters, but one had to stake what one had. Were they not pledged to sacrifice their lives for the souls of their fellow-men, all their worldly goods for the lives of others, not merely their superfluities but also what was necessary for their very existence? Did He spare Himself, when He came to sacrifice Himself for us? ... And as they had heard from their friends, the secular authorities at Pressburg were opposing the project with all their might, was not that in itself a sign that the arch-enemy realized that the banners of the Lord were on the march?

By Christmas, the new school was opened at the foot of the mighty castle-rock of the old Danube fortress. Pupils arrived in throngs, and conversions were swift and easy, for the child-like exuberant nature of the people had never really warmed to the chilling doctrines of Calvinism.

"Yes," said Mary, radiant with joy, to her Sisters, "Cardinal Pazmany is undoubtedly right: if Catholics only lived in accordance with their beliefs, the State could cheerfully grant religious freedom to all the others."

The head of the Holy Roman Empire, to be sure, was not of the same way of thinking, his motto being "compelle intrare," but he was exceedingly proud of the new Institute, frequently summoned the Mother General to private audiences, inviting her to tell him all about what she had already achieved and what she planned to do. On such occasions, she frequently met with Count Adolf Michael Althan, Imperial Field Marshal and Commander of the fortress of Raab, with whom Their Majesties frequently discussed the Counter-Reformation in Bohemia. The Count himself had returned but late in life to Holy Church. The conversion of his native country was a matter he had very deeply at heart, and he feared that his Imperial master's methods of going to work were all too rigorous. The slaughter that followed the Battle of the White Mountain was not yet forgotten, and the Court, he submitted, would do well not to rely too much on German arms. The spirit of revolt was still smouldering amongst the people, and though the nobles held their peace, it was with clenched fists and teeth. The hearts of the people were not to be cowed by edicts; all that edicts could do was to hinder the open progress of heresy, the *open*, be it well noted. Was His Apostolic Majesty aware of the many secret preachers who in the guise of itinerant journeymen, pedlers, and ballad-singers went from village to village propagating the new teaching?

"They must be prevented from doing any further harm," said Ferdinand coldly.

Count Althan, however, was not to be silenced thus. "How is it," he said, "that these people preach to such willing ears? It is because the hearts of the people and of our Bohemian people more than any other, crave for spiritual tidings. Does a hungry man when he sees food set before him ask whence it comes?—Or does anyone imagine that the iron sway of the Nuncio on the one hand, or the excesses of the Imperial troops on the other, who for years have been harassing the people, are likely to attract anyone to Holy Church? Are they not Catholics, too, at least in name, these Croats and Lombards, and these Spanish regiments whom the Duke of Friedland has been bringing into the country for the past two years? And yet what is the only personal experience

our people have of them but their profanity, their drink-
ing and looting, and things that one dare not even mention before the Reverend Mother here?"

"The Field Marshal is right," said Mary emphatically.
"It has always been a guiding rule for us in our work
to take from no one what he loves unless we give him
instead something he loves still better. More can be
effected by the use of kind and gentle words than by
those that are harsh and overbearing—for a troubled
dejected spirit will never love God perfectly nor do
much to His honour. It is only when men possess the
faith in joy and love, instead of obeying its behests in
the fear of an avenging justice, that all is well for the
holy cause. That is why a beginning should be made
when children are still very young; that is why it is more
important to give girls a Catholic education than to send
more regiments into a country to persecute fanatics and
poor preachers. For the Divine love is like a fire which
cannot be kept down, as it is impossible to love God
and not to labour to extend His honour."

"Bravo, bravo!" cried the Count. "In future, Reverend Mother, I shall go no more to listen to the Court
sermons of Father Lamormain, but you will find me
sitting at your feet whenever you choose to preach a
sermon. But now, seriously, when are you coming to
Prague to save His Majesty his three regiments, as you
said just now? I'll make you a present of a house on the
Kleinseite and enough for the upkeep of thirty persons."

Was it just a temptation, or was it a prompting of the
Divine grace, Mary asked herself, torn by conflicting
emotions, as she left the castle with the Count's promise
in writing, graciously confirmed by His Majesty, safely
tucked away in her pocket. From the snow-covered
square, she could see the sanctuary lamp gleaming warm

with its promise of comfort through the open door of St. Michael's Church, so that irresistibly she allowed herself to be drawn to that silent Presence. Oh, Lord, dare I risk it? Was it not a sign from Thee that the Count just happened to be at Court to-day? Was it not something even more than a sign, was it not rather a dispensation, clear as any command, that ever since his last serious illness, he has felt convinced that his recovery was due to our own humble prayers, and has therefore shown such a touching interest in our work?

She continued her way home, down the Coal Market and across the Bognergasse in the direction of the Hof, where stood the big College of the Jesuit Fathers. Did Francis Xavier hesitate to go forth alone—alone, mark well, thou craven soul!—alone to a country, nay, a world, larger than Bohemia and Hungary, larger than the German Empire and England and Flanders and Italy all put together? Alone—but with Christ on his lips and in his heart. And what was more, he did succeed in conquering that appallingly vast territory for his Lord, for God loves gallant souls. Oh, fie, to say that anything appears hard to thee in the service of God, for to those who love all is light. It is only our own mistrust of God that ties, as it were, His hands so that He cannot bestow upon us His divine gifts and His blessing.

The sky was vibrant with the loud clamour of a multitude of bells; across the Freyung the school-boys came running to the College of the Scottish Benedictines. It had been monks from her own island who had been the first to bring these people the Faith.

"Englishmen were the first to bring the Gospel to our country; Englishwomen shall help us to preserve it," the Elector of Bavaria had said, when he presented them with their house at Munich.

Maybe God will accept what we are doing in expiation of the sins of our misguided people at home, for the blood and tears of the martyrs and confessors. How can we bargain and compute whether what we have to do is not going to cost us too much in sacrifice; how is it possible for us to refuse Him anything? My novices are too young, too weak, and the rising generation as yet too lacking in experience, my faithful Mother Rectrices assure me; the burden is all too heavy. Now why, I wonder, has this kind of thing of late become the fashion?

She stopped short in the dark and narrow alley through which she was passing. Just above her head, great curved bars of iron protected the big dark windows of an old house, and through the panes of the last one on the left gleamed ruby-red the light of a sanctuary lamp. Barely seventeen he had been, the little Polish Prince who had lived in that house a generation ago, and whose bedroom had now been converted into a chapel.

She found the gate unlocked and groped her way up the winding stairs and through the little door leading to the tiny costly sanctuary, gleaming and exquisite as the lining of a shell, with its golden garlands and delicate floral motifs painted on the panelling. The place where the bed had once stood, before which the little schoolboy had prayed and scourged himself, was now occupied by the little baroque altar, with its spirals, scrolls and volutes, and its chubby gilded cherubs. Mary smiled; even now it was a dwelling worthy of a young prince. There he had lain sick, that same little Stanislas, and his dissolute brother and the Lutheran landlord had refused to admit a priest to visit him. . . . Then Our Lady herself had come with St. Barbara and the high court of heaven, and they had brought him the Bread of Life, just as the

painting above the altar depicted it all so beautifully. . . .
And that delicate little pampered lad had found the
courage to break loose from his gilded prison and to
flee over mountains and rivers from the horsemen sent
out by his brother, until he had finally found the home
for which his heart was longing at Dillingen College.
And now behold him already raised to the altars, together
with austere Aloysius, who at the age of twenty-one
was also a saint of God. No, no matter how young you
were, you could serve God heroically and with all your
heart and strength. In that little jewel-casket of a chapel,
gleaming so peacefully in the flickering light of the
sanctuary lamp, long-forgotten memories suddenly came
back to her, memories of her own happy youth. Oh,
Babthorpe Park, oh, those secret watches in the Castle
chapel, oh, that fond soaring exaltation of the soul,
straining to heaven with fledgling wings! Mary knelt
down, covering her face with her hands as one picture
swiftly blotted out the other.—No, no, all the well-
meant advice of prudent, cautious folk was foolishness,
sheer foolishness and lack of vision. You had to think
heroically of others. And the hero in them grew in
stature, the more you invoked him with confidence. I
will invoke the heart of my youth within me, when I
feel my courage fail, together with the hearts of those
trusty Sisters of mine whom God gave me as my companions in those days of the past. How young we were
when we set out on our great adventure!—I will launch
that foundation at Prague . . . bestow your blessing on
my work, my little brother Stanislas; yes, you are my
brother, you know, for we, too, observe the Rule of
your great Father Ignatius, and we are going to a people
akin to your own, people of Slavonic blood as you were,
too, you holy little Prince.

N

Past the walls of the Ghetto she hurried along. It was the Sabbath and everything within was still. Then, her heart still full of Divine consolation, she crossed the Wipplingerstrasse along which a few coaches were still rolling towards the town hall, and so back to the *Stoss im Himmel*. The beehive cupola of her beloved church was now but a dim silhouette against the dusk of falling snow. Winefrid must leave Naples and come to Munich: she suddenly felt a violent longing to have her, the most faithful of her earliest comrades, with her again. Mary Poyntz should have the direction of the new house at Prague. Blissfully that night she fell asleep, setting out in her dreams on yet another voyage of adventure.

But it was not until May that Mary saw Prague for the first time, Prague, the enchanted city on the Moldau with its hundred towers. From the gardens of the Hradschin, white and purple lilac hung in luxuriant beauty over the high walls, and the nights on the Kleinseite were ablaze with fireworks and melodious with the music of serenades from the palaces of the nobility. Like a dark-walled island in their very midst stood the vast palace of the Duke of Friedland, most powerful and most hated of the Bohemian lords, who now lay far away in the north before the sea fortress of Stralsund.

Then it was June, and the lilacs faded, and in the Convent gardens of Strahov and of the Carmelite nuns, who guard the Infant Jesus in His stiff silken robes, lilies gleamed and the lime-trees were in blossom, and the whole city was full of their honeyed fragrance and the humming of bees. But the house of Count Althan with the fine big church still stood empty. Cardinal Harrach was raising difficulties and the nuncios were siding with him. A concentration of every energy on the work of Catholic reconstruction was what he, too, was after, and the Capuchins and Jesuits whom he had summoned to assist him were there for that purpose. But it was the old faith that was to be set up again, all the good old things that had been held in honour before the great ecclesiastical upheaval; the traditional element, despised by so many, was to be restored uncompromisingly to its former prestige. Bohemia, already divided against itself by the reformers, must tolerate no fresh sowers of dissension—not even if they came in Catholic garb. Nor, for the matter of that, Catholic women who led an adventurous life contrary to all accepted usage, who organized public schools for girls, passed themselves off as religious, and yet dispensed with the rule of enclosure. How could he hope to enforce a becoming respect for the decrees of the Council of Trent, were he to tolerate an Institute whose way of life was opposed to the express teaching of that same holy Council? In the times of rebellion and unrest, in which they were living, it was essential to strengthen the power of those in authority— how was he to be expected to recognize a community that did not even acknowledge his jurisdiction?

And the famous Father Valerio, the Capuchin preacher, who had been sent to the north from Milan by the Pope himself, so, as you might say, came straight from the fountain source, most strongly advised him to have nothing to do with them. What had he not heard in Rome on the subject of that impossible Institute! Ever since then he had considered it as something in the nature of a public duty to warn the faithful, and more especially the ecclesiastical authorities, against this fraud, and he had preached plenty of sermons in Italy to that same end. The Institute was nothing more nor less than heresy in disguise, a self-glorification of women, such as the Church had ever refused to countenance, a contempt of authority, dangerous exaltation, and a mania for spiritual adventure. And if all this had already been the case in Rome and Italy, how much more was to be expected in countries where the old faith was exposed to peril from all sides, where even Catholic minds were already infected with the same fatal craze for innovation and sensation-mongering.

"What kind of sorry world is this where one thing that is good stands in the way of another that is also good?" said Mary sadly when she heard all this. It was as though a storm-cloud had suddenly gathered over the fair garden of her devoted labours, that at long last was just beginning to blossom. Ah, perhaps, too long, she had lost sight of that sinister menacing volcano in the background. . . . And now, once more, the ground was suddenly beginning to rock beneath her feet.

The Bishop of Eichstätt had in his diocese three hundred devout young women who had attempted to form themselves to an Ursuline community; the venture, however, had proved unsuccessful. His Grace now conceived the happy idea of offering these sheep without a fold to the Paradeiser Haus. They were to be admitted immediately as professed nuns, since it was assumed that they had already proved their vocation for the religious life by that initial experiment; in return, the Institute was to be allowed to take over the property of the community. Mary laughed rather grimly when she read Winefrid's horrified letter. That, forsooth, was an almost humorous answer to her prayers for new postulants. It was sheer madness to assume that she could afford, especially now, to impede her work with a flock of half-formed religious, already prepared to a totally different way of life.

Her refusal aroused such a storm in Munich that, for a space even the Paradeiser Haus seemed to totter in its foundations. A mercy that the Elector, at least, was to be relied on. The ecclesiastical notabilities of Munich, however, became markedly aloof, and families related to the rejected Ursulines were pleased to feel themselves affronted and aired their resentment by removing their daughters and nieces from the school.

They'll calm down in time, Mary surmised, and she ruled a line beneath the fatal letter, which signified that, as far as she was concerned, the matter was over and done with.

More disturbing, however, was the mail she received that same day from Vienna, from which she gleaned that the Archbishop of that city, the still very powerful Cardinal Khlesl, had suddenly begun to manifest unusual interest in her foundation in the Salvatorgasse. Two clerics attached to St. Stephen's had recently called to make a formal visitation of the premises and had asked for the Rule to be submitted for their perusal. They had also attended the recital of the Office, examined the list of the pupils, been present at several of the lessons, required the names and ages of the professed nuns and of all the other members of the household, and had finally drawn up an impressive report on the result of their investigations. What, Mary asked herself, was the meaning of all this. A line of communication, it would seem, had been established between Prague and Vienna. She read the letter through again, then suddenly gave a soft, but unmistakable whistle through her teeth. Aha, here we had it: "And Canon Schuchmayr said that it was but natural His Grace the Archbishop should wish to know what foundations were being made in his diocese. . . ." Sancta simplicitas! Was it possible that hitherto he had been left in ignorance? Had they not trustfully, and in all simplicity, presumed that the Court would pass the information on to all the other authorities? And it was quite possible that the Emperor, for his part, had imagined that his consent was all that was needed.

Mary had sufficient acquaintance of those in high places to know that the mere fact of forgetting to wait upon some dignitary or of omitting a ceremonial call might exact a long and heavy toll from the offender. She believed that she was not altogether wrong in the surmise that the difficulties she had had to cope with at Prague were mainly due to her having first visited the friends and kinsfolk of Count Althan in the great houses on the Kleinseite before paying her duty call at the archepiscopal palace. It had been an unpardonably foolish sin of omission. Alas, in close and constant contact with the wisdom of innocence and the generosity of youth, it was but too easy to forget the puerilities that grown-ups regard as inviolable laws.

And the Archbishop of Vienna, as Mary was very well aware, though a zealous, was also a masterful man. Monasteries and convents groaned beneath his iron rule, though he could show himself generous and indulgent enough towards those disposed to becoming docility. Freedom of election in the religious chapters was curbed with a strong hand. Only recently, he had reversed the election of a new abbot by the Scottish Benedictines, though made in all due form, and had inflicted on them the austere Prior of St. Emmeran. He had also acted in the same high-handed manner with the monks of St. Dorothea, for all the world as though exemptions for him were non-existent. Consequently, what must his feelings have been to have had a women's convent, entirely independent of his jurisdiction, founded beneath his very nose! And the case was aggravated even more, seeing that it was not only an ambition but also a pet enterprise of his to reorganize the indigent and moribund Sisterhoods of Vienna and to utilize them for the education of girls, though on old-fashioned lines, with strict enclosure both for Sisters and pupils. . . . Well, they could prepare themselves for some pretty developments.

And then, all of a sudden, rumours began to crop up everywhere that in Rome, too, the tide had turned against them. The Cardinals of Prague and Vienna had complained that their authority had been flouted and had asked for the necessary instructions—all of which might but too easily bring a wasps' nest about their ears, especially now that that fanatical Capuchin was moving up his obsolete artillery against them. . . . But the "Jerusalems" could do no more than God permitted they should do. It remained to be seen who came off best in the end.

Brother Ass, however, was again clamouring for attention, for Mary had had an alarming recurrence of her old malady. She found a veritable solace in the peace and quiet of the vast Bohemian forests surrounding the spa at Eger. It was a sultry late summer, the clearest days of the year. In ever-deepening tints of blue, the mountain ridges and walls of forest lay one behind the other. In between, stood the sheaves on the fields where the harvest had been reaped, squatting there like gnomes, when the red moon sailed over the slumbering earth.

Strange, thought Mary, her weary heart lulled in that deep all-enveloping peace, strange that there were such things in the world as letters, finance, and outraged dignitaries. That there were some who still failed to grasp the real meaning of God—God always and God alone. That we could still go on thinking of things other than those He works within us and would have us do. "With the help of His grace," she resolved, "I will begin to amend my life, that I may be worthy to do what God in His immeasurable bounty and goodness would have done by me, and Our Lady shall assist me in this work of amendment. . . ."

Then, with renewed peace and clarity of purpose, she returned to the struggle. There were journeys to be made to Vienna, to Pressburg, to Munich, and everywhere she found the ground rocking slightly with tiny subterranean upheavals. Perhaps, she told herself, it would be best to make straight for the source of the trouble—Rome. Winefrid was frankly alarmed when she heard of this project. This time they would be bringing no advocate along with them to plead their cause, as they had hoped when last they had said farewell; all they had gained in the interval were new and dangerous enemies, and they would find themselves entangled in a veritable network of accusations, of which as yet they were absolutely in ignorance.

"I know, Win," said Mary calmly, "that it's all my own fault. If only I had abstained from making those new foundations. Father Gerard once more has proved himself to have been in the right, and you, too, all of you, were perfectly right—it's my obstinacy alone that is to blame for everything. Yes, but it's no good crying over spilt milk; the least one can do is to clear up the mess. And that I can best do myself. The Holy Father, as you know, is well disposed towards me."

"Well, what are we going to do?" asked Winefrid with a worried air. She knew her friend and leader only too well. None could solicit the opinion of others more humbly and sincerely than she; the very youngest of her Sisters was at perfect liberty openly to speak her mind. On such occasions, Mary would give each and every one a respectful, nay, even a grateful hearing, after which she would do precisely what she thought best, even if it meant at the risk of her very life. And an expedition to Rome at that juncture might easily mean the exaction of that price. The cure at Eger appeared to have benefited her mentally rather than physically, for the malady that befell her now with such startling suddenness was something hitherto unknown to her physicians. She found herself, all at once, unable either to stand or to lie down, and could only crouch in her armchair, shaken with agonizing paroxysms of pain. She had to be rocked like a baby to enable her to get a little sleep, and she found it impossible to keep any food down. It was pathetic to see her signing for the little table with her papers to be brought to her bedside during the intervals between her attacks, when she would then dictate, or even herself write a line at a time before relapsing into a kind of semi-consciousness.

It was a sad Christmas for the Paradeiser Haus. The children tiptoed through the long corridors, for they all knew that the Reverend Mother was very, very ill; the Sisters went about with eyes red with weeping, and every day a messenger arrived with inquiries from the Elector and his consort. When night came, a heavy footstep softly made its way up the stairs, and it was no unusual thing for Lennard to spend the whole night, wrapped in his cloak, on her threshold, as once in years gone by in the Italian inns, only with his rosary in his hand in the place of the pistol of yore, and his faithful heart rent with a strange, inarticulate sorrow.

But on New Year's Day, such a cry of dismay went up from the Paradeiser Haus, that one might well have thought the Swedes were already in sight, for, when the community assembled at her bedside to proffer their pious wishes for the coming year, Mary had acknowledged them with a smile in the following words: "May Our Lord and His Blessed Mother receive your prayers at once for my safe journey, for at noon I am leaving for Rome.—One thing alone we ought to fear, and that is of being too easily afraid," she said to the horrified Sisters, declined civilly, but in a voice that brooked no contradiction, any further visits, and cut Winefrid's protests short with the calm rejoinder: "If you say another word against it, I shall leave you here."

Then she compiled a long list of instructions and dispositions for the coming weeks, sent a messenger over with a note to the Elector, and at three o'clock that afternoon, whilst a snow-storm was descending on Munich that seemed determined to bury the entire city up to the tower-tops of Our Lady's Church, her litter passed through the Isar Gate, escorted by two Sisters and her two faithful friends.

*   *   *   *   *

That journey was one long nightmare. Perhaps it was even worse for Mary's companions than it was for herself, for during the greater part of the time they never knew whether she were in the body or without, that poor tortured body, shaken and convulsed in unspeakable agonies, no longer capable of assimilating its tiny modicum of nourishment, for all the provision required for her on the journey was a little bag of oatmeal for gruel. It was as though she were tossed on a dark

stormy sea of pain, from which every now and then she
emerged like one who had returned, alien and dumb,
from a long, long journey. On such occasions, all that
she desired to know found voice in the ever-recurring
question: Where are we now? And each time her
white drawn face would be convulsed with a sharp
spasm of pain when she realized how slow a progress
they were making, encumbered as they were with a sick
woman and her litter on those difficult snow-bound roads.
During the few hours when she was conscious of her
surroundings, her mind pushed on ahead. How often
she had reached Rome since the Isar Gate was blotted
out behind them in a whirl of eddying snow, how often
knelt at the feet of the Holy Father, heard his voice
encourage her with kindly consoling words, how often
had she seemed to have the saving Decree in her very
hands . . . so vivid it all seemed to her that she could
almost feel the velvety dryness of the parchment, smell
the wax of the great seal. And they had not even yet
reached Innsbruck!

"I've given up worrying," said Winefrid to Father
Lee. "Our Lord must have revealed to her that she will
get to Rome, otherwise she would have been dead long
ere this."

All the same, it was almost more than one could bear
to listen to that soft, half-suppressed moaning that went
on for hours at a time behind the curtains of the litter.
The four faithful friends relieved one another at regular
intervals, not a word was exchanged on the subject, but
each one knew that during those brief intervals, the
mind needed relief every bit as much as the body. The
bearers, who were replaced by others at every halt along
the road, were sullenly convinced that the entire company belonged by rights in a madhouse, and that dragging

anyone more dead than alive across the mountains was nothing short of outrage. But they paid well, and for the rest, after all, it was their own business.

There were times, usually about evening, when Mary would suddenly return to consciousness. On such occasions, she was cheerful, even merry, talked volubly, asked questions, drew her companions out, and prayed with them, and it was hours like these that kept them going. But there were others, when she would seriously debate with herself whether she ought not to ask the faithful priest to administer Extreme Unction—her candle and shroud, as well she knew, travelled along with her, stowed away in her valise—but she also knew that any such request would mean the utter dismay of her poor Sisters. No, it was better for them not to know how hard that journey was along the very brink of eternity. . . . Had she not made a General Confession before leaving Munich? Had she not for many years received the Body of her Lord each time as though it were the last? Once, however, she deemed it advisable to give some necessary instructions—for, whatever happened, the journey to Rome must never be abandoned—"just in case" she were not to reach her goal. But one glance at the blanched faces before her told her that not one of them as yet was capable of even facing the idea—so she forced herself once more to laugh, a laugh that certainly rang very hollow, and to Elizabeth's startled query: Whether she really thought . . .? she was again only able to reply: "I know not whether it is Our Lord's good pleasure to work a miracle for me . . . though what does it really import whether I die in my bed or under a hedge, so long I be found faithful. . . . My Sisters, whether we live or die, we serve a good Master."

Then the strained look, the haunting anxiety in their faithful eyes would gradually relax, and as, with a patient smile she sank back on her hard pillow, the thought would come to her: "Sleep ye now and take your rest. . . ." Ah, faithful they all were, faithful, maybe, even unto death, but all the same, there was *not one* of them capable of gauging the situation with a cool clear eye, not one before whom she had not to play the part of the stronger woman. Each leant on the other; all had to be guided and consoled, all. The leader is always alone.

It was thus they reached Rome. From the street Mary was borne straight to her bed, to the first bed they could find in the old house that was still theirs, and which now stood tenantless. For three weeks she was obliged to keep her bed, but after the first week, during which she hovered in a semi-conscious state between life and death, Elizabeth had to seat herself at her bedside with paper, pen and ink, whilst Mary dictated for hours at a time, brooking not the slightest interruption. Thus was evolved a long and circumstantial account of twenty long years, of her way of life, her work, and her experiences. The Holy Father was to know all, was to be in a position to survey all, and thus be enabled to judge things for himself. What need for her to stoop to give as much as a passing mention to baseless rumours and accusations? Her life in actual fact was a better refutation than any polemics.

In the early days of March Mary was received in audience.

After she had gone, the Holy Father paced the room for some time in silence. He was thinking of the strange woman who had just knelt before him, worn to a shadow, her face little more than two great burning eyes, and how, humbly as any child, she had asseverated her complete submission to his will—"he had but to command, she would obey him blindly, would not oppose him by as much as a single word, even though it pleased him to destroy all that she had built up in so many arduous years"—and how on the other hand, she had steadfastly insisted that she had acted in obedience to a divine inspiration. What was he to make of it all? Was it merely yet another manifestation of the fanaticism that was blazing up everywhere in that hapless age of wild unrest? No doubt she was a saintly woman, but her scheme was as irrational, as contrary to all sane thinking, to the whole concensus of tradition and to the cool judgment of canonists and ecclesiastical politicans as it was also repugnant to the simple pious feeling of a Catholic people. . . . The matter would again have to be assigned to a special Congregation of Cardinals: more than that she could scarce expect. These interminable Memorials were not the right way of going to work—impossible to read them oneself, and the prelates had no time for reading them either. She would have to condense the whole thing once more and hand over the document to two personages on the Commission already familiar with the accusations that had been brought against her—he himself had never gone into the matter more closely, it was the business of the Propaganda to deal with it, *de minimis non curat praetor*—in any case, it appeared to be extremely complicated. After that, we should have to see. . . .

"He would not even read our beautiful Memorial," said Mary to the Sisters, considerably dashed in her hopes.

All those pages, written with her heart's blood—confession, credo, jubilant thanksgiving in one—all had been written in vain, and had now to be reduced to a cut and dried summary of paragraphs and dates. And her new judges were themselves on the side of the enemy—the protector of the English clergy, who for that very reason would not be likely to quarrel with his clients on their account, and the General of the Society of Jesus, who would be the first to disclaim any connection with the Institute, who had already most emphatically denied the ever-recurring rumours that his Order was in any way connected with that foundation or had any kind of interest in it. Her judges could not have been more unfortunately selected. Or, was it possible that the choice had been made intentionally?

She lodged a formal protest with the Pope, but to bring Urban VIII from any decision, once he had made up his mind, was a task that would have reduced many a more skilful diplomat than Mary to despair.

"When it means relying solely on the justice of men in a matter running counter to their personal interests," she remarked to Winefrid with a bitter little smile, "then you realize for the first time how much that justice is worth. . . . *Omnis homo mendax*. Not one keeps either what he or his office promises. But should we, I wonder, be any different, Win mine?"

The Pope really did mean well with her. The amazing tenacity with which this woman returned again and again to battle for her practically lost cause made a strong appeal to the Caesar in his nature. She should have her chance, even though it meant defying every established precedent. She should be allowed to plead her own cause, if, in her incredible simplicity and, firmly convinced of her divine mission, she had omitted to secure or failed to discover an advocate to plead in her behalf. She should face her judges, an entirely new Council, and tell them exactly what she had in mind. She was not the type of person who could defend herself behind a rampart of legal documents. Of course, there had been that talk last July of a Decree of Suppression that was to reach the Bishops by way of the nuncios . . .? Was it not just about the time when the Cardinals of Prague and Vienna had lodged a complaint on the subject? Nothing further had been heard about it, so no doubt the papers were stowed away in the pigeon-hole of somebody's writing-table, gradually amassing a thick coat of dust. If the Decree were not already promulgated, this last supreme effort might end in scotching it for good and all. And even, were the Congregation, despite that effort, to confirm it, then at least she would have had a great, not to say, unique opportunity of restating her case.

To Mary it was all like a dream—like one of those strange adventures which, when the sleeper awakes, seem to have been but a mirrored reflection of some distant reality experienced long ago. The warm March sunlight on the gardens and fountains, the rigid figures of the Guards in their brilliant uniforms, the soft crunching of the sand beneath her feet; then the marble columns of interminable galleries, with always the double footfall of her steps and Winefrid's, who accompanied her to the door—it was like one of those plays which her little girls performed in Vienna and Munich, all as though it had been rehearsed before; how they clasped hands and Winefrid said: "God bless you!"—after which a curtain was swept back. Then a mosaic floor gleamed, blurred and dim in the subdued light, and the white steps leading up to the raised seats had a reddish glow from the purple robes of the assembled prelates, conspicuous amongst them the black and white Dominican habit of Cardinal

Scaglia. Somebody was reciting a string of sonorous Latin phrases; it was Cardinal Borgia, who presided. After that, he made a sign for her to begin.

As though through a mist, Mary saw the long Capuchin beard of Cardinal Barberini and found herself thinking in surprise: How white his beard has grown. For a moment she seemed to glimpse the great brown faces of the sunflowers that had nodded over a similar discussion many years ago—and then she heard herself beginning to speak. If only her voice did not play her false; for some days past she had been troubled with a racking cough and that morning had patiently swallowed all the syrups and soothing mixtures that Anna Grunwald had carefully stowed away in their baggage . . . but it was all right, her throat was not troubling her in the least. She seemed to hear herself talking from somewhere very very far away. Occasionally she was aware, with a kind of detached astonishment, that she was making little gestures with her right hand to emphasize some point or other, noticed, too, that the cuff of her sleeve was getting very threadbare, and heard herself saying: "... neither do I wonder that Holy Church makes difficulty in approving a thing so new; contrariwise I do profoundly reverence that vigilancy of theirs. . . . For ten years my companions and I endeavoured to ascertain the will of God regarding our vocation, and the hardships and sufferings we endured in that uncertainty were so great that I esteem all the sicknesses and afflictions that I have suffered since the time when it pleased God to reveal to me His will as child's play and I could not imagine that in future anything worse could befall me. . . . And I seek no other renown but to be found in the hour of my death faithful to God. If therefore His Holiness and Your Eminences thought it good that I

O

should desist, I should at once humbly submit to your decision as the will of God to me: but I could not in fidelity to Him change my plan or undertake another in its room. I place myself entirely in your hands."

There was a slight rustling sound as the man in the Preacher's habit bent towards the Capuchin. Cardinal Borgia sat there leaning his head on his hand, whilst the Prefect of the Papal Household listened without moving a muscle.

The sunlight shifted and the group beneath the scarlet canopy glowed like the heart of a crimson rose. Mary heard her voice going on: "So the will of God is fulfilled in me and my companions, I am content. I and mine are in no haste, what is not achieved in one year can be achieved in another. I can wait for God Almighty's time and His good pleasure, for it is meet for man to follow God, not hasten heedlessly before Him. . . ."

Then that ordeal, in its turn, was over.

"I hold," Cardinal Borgia was saying an hour later to Pope Urban, "that this her cause is of God, and that I neither can nor durst be against it. But my power is not enough to assist it, such and so powerful are her enemies. Therefore I humbly entreat Your Holiness that I may deal no more in it."

"We are returning to Munich," Mary announced that evening to her Sisters. "My work here is done. Do not, I beg of you, make my heart heavier, otherwise I must conclude that your solicitude is concerned solely with my poor brother, the body, with this good-for-nothing head, and not with my dearest child, our sacred cause. We have no money, Winnie? Well, I have found out a good way to make our monies hold out on our journey: as long as we deny to no poor body an alms who shall ask

it on the road, we shall assuredly be welcome guests at
Our good Lord's table."

*   *   *   *   *

It seemed strange to be again in Munich, back again
in a city, after the long weeks on the road. Their last
journey had been really enjoyable, just as though it had
tried to compensate them for all the horrors of that
wintry trek to Rome. Mary's health seemed to be
improving, and the last weeks, once they had left the
Alps behind, and were floating down the Inn in the
radiant June sunshine, had been, day after day, so many
gifts of God. Mountains, stars, fleecy-clouded moonlit
nights, early sunrises beneath a still, unsullied sky, foaming cascades wafting veils of spray from red rocks,
flaming Alpine roses covering water-worn rocks with
their luxuriant growth, villages nestling in their valleys
as though in the hand of God; it seemed hardly credible
that for the last eleven years there had been war in the
land. Hardly credible that that sinister threat from the
north was drawing ever closer. And hardly credible
that the cause so sacred and dear to one's heart had in
far-away Rome received its quietus with a few strokes
of the pen, as though one had never set out on that all-
but fatal journey at Christmastide to stake one's all on
a last card.

On the great highway, life seemed oddly detached
and without desire; you almost forgot what was important and what was unimportant; you began to understand the eternal pilgrims and all the roving folk who,
to the horror of all good burghers, had succumbed to its
enchantment, and who roamed the world in the wind
and the rain, without settled abode or journey's end. . . .

It was, indeed, high time that we got back to work again, was Mary's concluding remark to Winefrid, who had listened to all the foregoing with very wide open eyes, without exactly appreciating its sentiments.

But it was as though one had lost the habit of shouldering burdens during that long interval of suspense, hovering between two posts of duty. Or did it only seem so, just because misfortunes were now crowding down on them, thick and fast? For this was now the story of holy Job and his messengers all over again. How many couriers of ill tidings, all unbeknown to them, must have posted past them on their journey home? The house at Naples, that had served as novitiate for so many a long year, had been dissolved. The Archbishop had delayed taking the inevitable step as long as he was able to evade the issue, but, he was finally obliged, albeit with the greatest reluctance, to carry out the duty imposed upon him. . . . Novices and professed were to return to their own country and kinsfolk. The memorial of the aristocracy, "that as, by the grace of God, we have so many helps for men, this, the only one for women, may not be wanting," had been dismissed. A letter had been addressed to the Pope by the people of Naples asking whether they were aware in Rome that the return of the Sisters to their native-land was rendered impossible owing to the penal laws. Were there not among their number young women little more than children and many sick persons who had worn themselves out in their work for the school—what was to become of them all? And the burden of responsibility would eventually rest with the citizens of Naples, should the Decree for their expulsion really pass into effect.

"The letter is well worded," said Mary with sombrely knitted brows; "it now but remains to be seen whether it will reach its destination."

For Mary Poyntz insisted that letters had been dis-
appearing in the mails in the most mysterious way, and
that the seals of others had obviously been tampered with.
Spies were evidently at work again.

Well, what's the next item?—Letters from Flanders,
God help us! The Liége foundation seemed destined to
remain her chief cross, just as though the restless spirit
of the unhappy Praxedes still walked there.

"Oh, so they have again been trying to make their
own future security doubly sure by taking steps to emanci-
pate themselves from me altogether and to introduce a
'mitigated' rule, together with enclosure under the
bishop's jurisdiction!" Had these women gone crazed?
How was the Holy See ever going to approve an Institute divided against itself?—Would any bishop ever
trust a community that had cast off its head and was
merely intent on saving its own skin? Write, Elizabeth,
write. . . . So they were so very much afraid that
they were going to be suppressed, were they? Had
anything ever been said about the northern houses
being threatened with dissolution? Why, as much as
four years ago, was I not already of the Cardinals'
opinion that we must needs abandon our work in the
south since a people whose faith had never been imperilled
could never hope to understand us, but that, on the other
hand, there was very different work awaiting us on the
battle-fields of the north. Write and tell them that this
fear that is urging them to dissension and desertion has
no other basis than idle gossip, calculated—and, as we see,
not without good reason—to play upon their womanish
fears, in order to force them to concessions. . . . Write
them that our trusty ones have to be prepared for very
different things; the so-called Decree of Suppression
lacks any solid foundation—otherwise, is it likely that

the Cardinals in Rome, who are well-disposed in my regard, would not have said a word about it during the time I was in Rome? Consequently whatever is ordained on the authority of any such mandate, may in no circumstances be accepted by any of our members. They are to excuse themselves with all due modesty and respect, and are to give as their reason that they had heard from me that the author of that Decree was not favourably disposed towards our Institute; that it had been drawn up on his own responsibility without any mandate from His Holiness and without the full knowledge and consent of the other Cardinals entrusted with the conduct of this affair. Should the Bishops and Nuncios see fit to pronounce sentence of excommunication (which I do not consider likely), so be it; it should not be difficult for us to find redress. It behoves our associates to serve the Institute and to suffer persecution for its sake, though we should be inclined to consider any such proceeding as one of exceptional rigour.

"My sister, Elizabeth Ward, is amongst the renegades? You say she tore my portrait to pieces and trod it underfoot?"

Mary sat very still. Elizabeth Cotton softly slipped out of the room to fetch a taper, for twilight had already descended on the house.

That winter it would be six years since Barbara died. The letter announcing that Elizabeth had entered the Institute was her last happiness on earth. . . .

"Maybe it was not through malice they erred, and will repent them later on," she said gently to Elizabeth Cotton, who tiptoed her way back with the candle, looking unhappy and ill at ease.

All the same, during the rest of that evening, Mary could not bring herself to address Elizabeth by name. . . .

"Winefrid will have to leave for Liége at once and take the letters with her—I'd have liked her to have a little rest, but there's far too much at stake. And I myself must go to Vienna; we have no Nuncio here, and it is absolutely necessary I should know what messages come in from Rome."

*   *   *   *   *

Hitherto, thank God, the Vienna foundation had been spared. Never a cloud had obscured the sunlight of the Imperial favour. Cardinal Khlesl seemed to be more kindly disposed towards them, even to the extent of sending flowers for their May altar. That, to be sure, had been some time ago, but still. . . . The school was doing well. Helen Clifford's girls might proudly challenge comparison with the Jesuits' boys. They actually got up Latin plays for private performance—the martyrdom of Our Lord's holy bride, St. Cecily, and similar edifying subjects, adapted for such occasions by Mother Geneviève, all the elegant costumes for these productions being turned out by the sewing class. Court ladies, accustomed to Italian operas and English players, had been most generous with their applause, and had followed up the theatricals by regaling the girls with a dainty collation. New books had been purchased for the library, and, for the kitchen, the very latest thing in turning-spits, which saved a lot of work. To think that there were still such little things in the world to preoccupy one and to be glad about!

Mary plunged into that tranquilly busy life, so absorbed in its all-important little affairs, as into a soothing and friendly element. So long it had been a stranger to her. How remote it all seemed to her now—the highroads

with their terrors and their pageantry; remoter still the
Roman Curia, the antechambers of Cardinals, the great
Roman sanctuaries. How long ago they seemed, those
arduous journeys to launch some new foundation, those
interminable negotiations with generous but obstinate
gentlemen, and devout but vain-glorious ladies, whose
wishes could never be deferred to enough, unless, in the
twinkling of an eye, you wished to transform your
patrons into dangerous enemies. All that was now a
thing of the past. Here one day was just like the other.
Early in the morning—and the mornings were already
getting autumnally dark—you wended your way to Maria
Stiegen, whilst the housewives were hurrying off to
market, basket on arm, their drowsy eyes beneath their
high coifs still heavy with sleep. Then the girls would
begin to arrive in swarms, chattering and giggling, a
good many in sedan-chairs, some even in their own
coaches, the majority escorted by some relative or maid.
The house was soon full of life and buzzing like any bee-
hive.

Mary sat in her room overlooking the steep Salvatorgasse, through which she could just glimpse the high
roof and the lovely bell-turret of the church. She was
reading letters from the various houses of the Institute,
dictating, and saying her prayers. For the first time for
many months, she was finding the leisure to peruse and
docket notes taken years ago of spiritual exercises and to
draw up rules of conduct and instructions for her
daughters, leisure to retire to the little oratory and
to devote long hours to meditation. Sometimes there
would come a knock at the door, as she sat there busy
with her papers, and in response to her "Ave," some
senior girl would enter, or maybe one of the many
young novices who had come over from England and

who (owing to the unrest in Flanders) had been sent on by Winefrid to Munich or Vienna. Then, with flushed cheeks, timid downcast eyes, and nervous fidgeting fingers, the young thing would seat herself on the round stool at Mary's feet, and in faltering words would seek guidance in all those little problems which loom so large in the initial stages of the spiritual life. . . . How did one acquire a true devotion to the Holy Ghost, and what penitential exercises were most acceptable to God? How did one obtain sisterly love and that spirit of recollection that as yet left so much to be desired? How did one discipline a certain touchiness and a sharp tongue . . . and might one be permitted to go to confession to the Franciscan Father who had preached the other day at Maria Stiegen, and who was assuredly a chosen servant of God, for his words had made one feel so truly contrite. . . .

When after kissing her hand and dropping a deep curtsey, they had finally taken their leave, very red about the ears, Mary would gaze long in the direction of the door that had just closed behind them. . . . Children, fortunate, thrice-happy children, who still thought that the Imitation of Christ consisted in things such as these. . . . What more blissful than that spring-tide of first love in the spiritual life . . . and could it be that she had once known it too? Happy children, who could still give utterance to the thoughts that oppressed them—Would she ever be able to capture the secret again?

Ever since her last visit to Rome, something seemed to have snapped within her, she knew not what. All she knew was that the strong tide of grace that had hitherto borne her up through every storm and persecution had suddenly dried up, and that her way now lay over barren rocks beneath a lowering sultry sky, behind which, im-

measurably remote, God hid Himself in silence. What·
had she done to make Him turn His face from her?
She had been found faithless, incapable of guarding that
which had been committed to her care; like a death-
doomed ship it was drifting to destruction—with all on
board, all those faithful, trusting souls—any day now the
end might come, then all would crash to ruin, and the
others would be the ones to suffer. And who was to
blame? She, she alone. God did not demand what was
impossible; He had given her loyal and wise counsellors
to assist her in her work. Everything might have been
saved; it was her over-weening pride alone that had stood
in the way. Had she ever lent ear to the advice of others?
Had she ever deferred to others' opinions? Before her
lay those pages which fourteen years ago at St. Omer
she had scribbled all over with good resolutions and
pious aspirations, no doubt at the time of their spiritual
exercises. . . . Yes, then everything had seemed possible;
she had deemed herself to be on the right road, as
probably she was, and God had not been sparing, either
with His grace or inner light. . . . And to-day? Had
there ever been in their time a call such as hers? A call
to propagate the new way of life to God's greater glory
in the sight of men and angels? When, through her
own folly, had she lost that grace? When had her path
strayed from the one straight road? Alas, she knew not.

She only knew that the inner light, the perennial joy
that had illumined her path through thick and thin,
had been extinguished, utterly extinguished, and she
believed that because of her pride, her recklessness, her
negligence, her unpardonable shortcomings, her great
and holy work had been brought to the verge of ruin.
And the Lord spake to the wicked steward: Out of thy
own mouth I judge thee. . . . Ah, had she not thought

in the pride of her heart to bring the Lord a thirty, sixty, nay, a hundredfold harvest for the seed that had been sown? And now the fields stood high, but she knew that relentlessly the storm-clouds were bearing down upon them. She had been found wanting, faithless to her trust. Counted, weighed in the balance, and found wanting. ... Years ago I used to pray that God would let me die if I were not worthy to carry on the work—God has let me live. Was that His punishment?

The Sisters were greatly edified by the touching zeal with which the Mother General associated herself with their daily tasks. She helped the novices at their work, served at table, washed the dishes in the scullery, and folded the linen. Unsmilingly, she went about it all: to her it seemed that all day long she ought by rights to be on her knees, begging their forgiveness that she was even there, that she had entered their lives, had linked their lives to hers, was set over them in authority. When, after proffering some request or receiving some little instruction, novices left her room, she would sometimes, laboriously and painfully, kneel down and in humble atonement kiss the floor where their feet had stood, telling herself in bitter humility: "These children are still innocent, burning with holy zeal, and free from all grave sin. And I? What have I made of my soul since the days when I was as young and as unsullied as they?"

When her mind reverted to that last journey to Rome, that terrible journey hovering between life and death, she shuddered in sheer horror. "Was I mad? Had sickness undermined my reason? How should I ever dare now to appear before my Judge?—Lord, O Lord, be patient a little longer!"

Thus Advent passed in unspeakable desolation, nor

did Christmas bring the faintest glimmer of light into
the darkness of her tortured heart. Ever since All Saints,
the holy old Carmelite and friend of the Emperor and
Empress had been resident in Vienna in the capacity of
Papal Legate. Perhaps he might be able to help her, only
that she seemed to have lost the habit of words, of discussing her own miserable soul, which seemed hardly
worth troubling a saint about.

It was only about Epiphany, when she had finally
made up her mind to break this dreadful silence at any
cost and had dragged herself to the Palace, that she heard
that her old friend was sick unto death. She was admitted,
but there were many people, all strangers to her, standing round the bed, and Father Domenico looked so sadly
changed that she could not have found it in her heart to
trouble him, even had she been alone. The aged Carmelite was still able to recognize her, and with a feeble
hand he made a beckoning sign to the tall black-veiled
woman, before whom the others respectfully made way. .
Then, in the Spanish that was still familiar to her from
the days at St. Omer, he murmured the words: "The Dark
Night . . . yes, the Dark Night . . . the Divine Majesty
be praised."

She bowed her head in silence, then found her way
out again down the long staircases and endless corridors. Just as she was crossing St. Stephen's Churchyard,
the air was filled with the wild clamour of bells and she
told herself: Now the Saint is dead.

Late that night, she suddenly recalled that to the Carmelite the Dark Night signifies a state of the soul vouchsafed by a special grace of God—but the thought brought
her no consolation. Everything seemed infinitely remote,
indifferent. The best thing to do, she decided, would be
to creep softly down to the kitchen, late as it was, and

clean the long row of shoes she knew would be standing there, little shoes and big shoes, the shoes of the boarders and of the Sisters. That, at least, would be making herself really useful, far more useful than by the many futile words she had wasted on bishops and princes, and for which one day she would be called to give an account.

That all her eloquence had really been so much waste of breath, grew clearer and clearer to her with every day. Calling at the Nuncio's palace, she was very plainly given to understand that very dangerous moves were being contemplated in Rome.

"So one of these days you may live to see me buried with the carrion," she told the Sisters one evening during the recreation. "It's no laughing-matter, you know, to find yourself in the black books of the Holy Office. . . ."

One of the younger nuns began to cry, exclaiming between her sobs: "I could almost take it unkindly at the hand of God. . . ."

"If you thought so," said Mary almost harshly, "it were impossible for me to love you, and beware not to let such a thought come into your mind again."

But privately she thought: "If that were the worst that came into mine, oh, how happy I should be!"

The Decree appeared in due course, but the Emperor would not permit it to be promulgated in his dominions. Their Majesties were faithful subjects of the Church in all pertaining to their souls' salvation. But when, owing to a stupid mistake, for which some Papal Protonotary would eventually be held responsible, our latest and most valuable instrument for the restoration of the Faith was to be sacrificed, and that, as far as our own dominions were concerned, without the slightest ostensible reason, then the power of the Imperial protectorate would be

found to be valid, even against a Roman Decree. Mary
was given to understand that she could remain in Vienna
without fear, both Cardinal Khlesl and Father Lamormain
upholding the Emperor's decision. There was not a
soul in Vienna who would harm a hair of her head.

Whether she would not be equally safe at Munich?
she demurred.

The Bishop's secretary shook his long head somewhat
dubiously. "The Elector of Bavaria," he said, "is
known to be inclined to scrupulosity. It would be
surprising for him, even in a matter of minor importance, to set his face against a Roman decree, even
though it involved a member of his own illustrious
house."

"I see," said Mary, and thanked him for the information.

With a fast-beating heart she hurried through the
Rotenturmstrasse and crossed the High Market. There
was a twinkling of Sabbath lights and the sound of
strange chanting as she passed the Jews' Alley. The
thick snow glimmered blue-white on the little square.
She found the Sisters already at their evening meal, and
duly performed her penance for being late. Then she
announced to the Superior of the house: "I shall be
leaving to-night by the last mail for Linz."

—Into Thy hands I commend myself, O Lord!

*   *   *   *   *

On arriving at Munich, she was obliged to take to her
bed owing to a sharp attack of her old malady, brought
on by her too precipitate journey. From there she
indited a brief circular letter to all the houses of the
Institute. When the Bull appeared, which was now to

be expected any day, Elizabeth Cotton was to send the letter off at once and pledge all the Sisters to unconditional obedience. All that she herself could now do was to await developments.

It was the Friday after Candlemas. Mary was reciting Vespers with Mary Poyntz and her secretary when the Sister on duty at the wicket knocked at the door. Dean Golla of Our Lady's Church and two of his priests wished to see her.

"I cannot very well go to the parlour," said Mary, "as it isn't heated. Ask the gentlemen to be good enough to walk up."

She sat in her old arm-chair, close to the little Dutch stove, with a big shawl with a long fringe over her shoulders.

The Dean paused in the doorway and crossed himself. The Sisters rose to invite him in, but Mary stopped them with an abrupt gesture.

Without any form of greeting, the old gentleman unfolded a sheet of paper and set about the task of reading the contents—cleared his throat with obvious embarrassment, then began in a voice that was none too steady: "You are to arrest the person of Mary Ward as a heretic and schismatic and instigator of revolt against the Holy See."

What followed after that, nobody heard. The Sisters flung themselves on their knees and clung to their beloved Mother, while the Canons remained like a couple of sticks in the doorway looking intensely uncomfortable. Scarlet in the face, and hardly pausing for breath, the Dean, however, floundered on miserably through the rest of his document, concluding his recital with the piteous entreaty: "Reverend Mother, I beg you won't make this accursed business more difficult

for me than it already is, otherwise I shall be forced to
resort to the secular authorities. . . ."

"That trouble shall be spared you," said Mary with
a smile; "it would ill become me to offer resistance. I
will willingly go to whatever prison you desire."

The more ignominious, the better. Heretic, schismatic! The very words were like so many blows. But,
then, there was so much to atone for, more than they
could ever know. . . .

All that she said, however, was: "Is the Elector
apprised of this?"

Yes, the Decree had arrived on the Feast of St. Sebas-
tian. "It's not really so bad as it sounds," the aged prelate
assured her lamely; "you'll only have to live in honour-
able seclusion at the *Anger* Convent—the Sisters, as you
know, are in excellent repute. We can even arrange for
the—er—removal to take place by night and thus spare
you any public dishonour."

Mary shrugged her shoulders. "Why talk of honour,
Your Reverence, when you brand me a heretic and treat
me as such? Things being as they are, what becomes of
my honour is of little account. For the rest, I thank you
for your offer, but not at any price will I avail myself
of it. The more widely all this is known, the better. It
would be doing myself an injustice to seek obscurity. . . .
But the gentlemen are still standing in the doorway!
Pray forgive me. Mary, my child, now don't make a
scene, but run and get two more chairs and a tankard of
wine. I presume I may be permitted to offer you some
trifling hospitality for the last time?"

And before they themselves knew what had happened,
they were actually sitting sociably together, whilst
Elizabeth poured out wine with a shaking hand and
proffered macaroons. "This woman a heretic!" mused

the younger of the two priests silently. "They might just as well give me a taste of the thumbscrews if they expect me to believe that. But orders are orders. There must be some terrible mistake somewhere, and, by St. Anne, I'd not care to have to answer for it on the Day of Reckoning!"

Whether the order had come from Rome, Mary was inquiring. "I doubt whether His Holiness has been apprised of it," she continued. "I wrote him just before leaving Vienna, and he is well disposed towards me. The Institute would be pure gold, he told me only the last time I was with him, if only it had enclosure." Had the Reverend Dean ever been to Rome?

No, but the Dean knew Cardinal von Zollern. And he had a picture in his possession that had rested on the Apostles' tomb in St. Peter's.

Mary embarked on reminiscences: she talked of the churches and the holy places, the Scala Santa and the Catacombs, until the twilight faded into darkness and the panes of the window shone blue-black in the tiny room.

"And now I suppose we'd better be moving," she said suddenly without a trace of embarrassment. "I must not keep the gentlemen too long"—and with a start of horror, they suddenly remembered the errand on which they had come.

"I presume I am permitted to take my leave of the community? No, better not?—Just as you wish. But I suppose there is nothing against my taking leave of my cell and once more commending myself here to my Lord."

She knelt down, the others following her example. The two Sisters were now weeping uncontrollably, and the priests were breathing with some difficulty. Then

P

silently she rose and moved to the door. The Dean had
ordered a coach, and Anne Turner was permitted to
accompany the sick woman to minister to her needs.

For some time past they had been expecting the notori-
ous heretic at the Poor Clare Convent of the *Anger*.
The Abbess was extremely upset and annoyed about it
all. Whatever, she thought, were they going to do
with such a person in the ordered routine of their peaceful lives? Strict orders had been given for a guard to
be posted day and night before a door, chained and
double-locked. No Sister was to be permitted to
exchange a single word with the prisoner or any written
communication, and what services were absolutely indispensable were to be carried out in complete silence under
pain of excommunication. The Franciscan Guardian was
waiting to receive the prisoner with a couple of sturdy
lay-brothers, for it was as well to be prepared for all
eventualities: tears, hysterics, scenes of violence were
what was to be expected from crazed women of that type.

Then, suddenly, a coach was heard to draw up outside;
the door of the enclosure creaked hesitatingly in the
silence, and they saw before them on the threshold a
smiling woman, very pale and leaning heavily on the
arm of a young lay Sister. With a profound reverence
she approached the Abbess and in a quiet well-controlled
voice begged pardon for the inconvenience she was
causing, promising to do her utmost to be of as little
trouble as possible. The Sisters stared at her in open-
mouthed amazement. Mother Katherine, who in the
world had been a Countess Bernardin, dropped a deep
curtsey, as in her younger days at the Court of Vienna,
words failing her altogether; the Franciscans were visibly
moved.

"You pity me?" said Mary quickly, and a strange smile flitted over her face. "Am I not being treated like a saint—I? Suffering without sin is no burden."

A small door stood open at the end of the passage. With a hand that trembled, and still unable to articulate a single word, the Abbess made a gesture of invitation. Slowly the prisoner passed down the corridor, then on the threshold of the cell, turned and with a smile bowed silently once more to the Sisters, who, with flickering dripping candles, lined the passage as far as the darkened staircase. After which, the Papal delegate double-locked the door and put up the chain.

Anne Turner struck a light, and discovered a bit of tallow-candle stuck in a bottle on the window-sill. She lighted it with some difficulty, for everything struck extremely damp.

"This, I should imagine, has once been the sick-room," was Mary's dry comment, when the feeble glimmer lighted up the tiny room. "Ours at home is somewhat cleaner, eh, my Jungfrau?"

A straw mattress lay on the floor in one corner, covered with a coarse woollen blanket, no doubt intended for Mary's attendant. In another corner stood a low bedstead with a deep sag in the middle, spread with sheets covered all over with curious-looking stains. The air was oppressive with a peculiar penetrating odour. Mary moved closer to inspect the bed.

"Why, it's still warm," she said in astonishment. "It would seem that some sick person has had to be dislodged on our account. Just hand me the light. To all appearances, the poor creature must have coughed up half a lung here over the bed and the floor—everything is sticky to the touch."

The windows, as she then discovered, were unfortunately almost entirely walled up, and there were mice too, judging by the state of the floor.

"Anne," she said, "I have certainly brought you to a palace."

Anne Turner, utterly aghast, still stood rooted to her corner.

"Well, well," said Mary, "the prison in which my good grandmother spent so many years was considerably worse than this. I remember how impressed I was as a child with the stick that had been gnawed all over by rats. And now, I think, we'll retire for the night. As I am the invalid, I'm going to sleep in this beautiful soft bed, and you will have to content yourself with the straw mattress.—What, you couldn't think of it? Mistress, you're not going to be dispensed from holy obedience as easily as you seem to imagine. The sick woman who inspires you with such revulsion was a human being like you and me—and possibly a better one at that."

There was a sound of fumbling with the bolts of the door. It groaned horribly on its hinges, then swung open into the passage. To their amazement, Mary and Anne Turner saw that four beds had been put up outside, doubtless for the Sisters on guard. On the threshold, however, knelt an aged Clare with hands upraised who with a beatific radiant smile, seemed to be gazing her fill of them like some worshipper before a shrine.

Then, slowly, the door clanked to again.

*   *   *   *   *

Night reigned in the cell, pitch-dark night, with the walls exuding a dank chill. There was a sound of rustling and gnawing as of busy mice, and the fetid odour from the bed seemed to pervade everything. To Mary it was as though the sheath of ice imprisoning her heart had melted, and with it that crushing burden that during the last months seemed to have frozen to a solid mass of pain.

Oh, the blessed sense of relief that the Lord had removed that burden with His own hands. Now her lot was patiently to endure and wait on His good pleasure, for the power of action had been taken from her. The words of the Compline psalm recurred to her, full of ineffable meaning: I cried unto the Lord with my voice: even unto God with my voice; and He gave ear to me. . . . In the day of my trouble I sought God, with my hands lifted up unto Him in the night: and I was not deceived. . . . My soul refused to be comforted. I remembered God and was delighted—and I mused: and my spirit swooned away. . . . Yes, thus it was indeed. . . . I was troubled and I spake not. . . . I thought upon the days of old: and I had in my mind the eternal years. . . . Oh, how hard it was to remember the days of grace of other years and to contemplate the approach of eternity. *Et dixi nunc coepi haec mutatio dexterae Excelsi!*[1] Yes, the hand of the Most High has intervened and brought this change to pass. I can make a fresh start. Into His hands I render the work that was beyond my feeble strength. May He carry it on; there are others better fitted for it than I. I have failed Him; nevertheless, I cast myself into the arms of His mercy. Even he who is vanquished may enter into His peace, so he has fought the good fight. And that I have done.

[1] And I said: Now have I begun: this change is of the right hand of the Most High.

Then suddenly before her closed eyes there flashed that inexorable interior light that she knew so well and the silent voice, before which every door was barred in vain, spoke to her in the silence: "What, you fain would rest before I give you leave? It is not enough to be content to endure as long as there is work still to be done. See to it that your imprisonment soon comes to an end, for there is still much fighting for you to do!" Ah, who is the great God like unto our God? He is the God that performs wonders. No prison door can bolt out His will. . . . He has made known His power among the nations: with His arm He has redeemed His people . . . the waters and the depths saw Him and were troubled. No, there is no evading His will. The empire of His will must be established. Lord, pardon my craven weariness! I wanted to see the victory gained, and therefore I grew faint-hearted, Thy path is over the earth and over the sea, and we see not the traces where Thy feet have passed, nevertheless it is our task to prepare the way that Thy will may be done. I will, I will; be Thou ever near me with Thy grace!

Softly she murmured the ever-comforting words of the eighty-fifth psalm: "For great is Thy mercy towards me, O Lord! and Thou hast delivered my soul out of the lower hell. O God, the wicked are risen up against me; and the assembly of the mighty have sought after my soul. . . . But Thou, O Lord, art a God full of compassion and merciful: long-suffering, and of much mercy, and true. Show me a token for good. . . ."

Infinitely at peace, she fell asleep, her heart overflowing with a long-forgotten happiness.

*   *   *   *   *

Mary awoke next morning refreshed after a profound sleep. Anne Turner had not closed her eyes all night, and dreaded even more the night to come, having just made the discovery that their cell looked out on to the convent burying-ground. "Nothing we learn in life, my Jungfrau," observed Mary, breaking in on her gloomy meditations, "is learnt in vain. Now I can thank God that the days of my youth were spent in the land of heresy. Now listen and mark me well: we are in urgent need of lemons for my sick-draught, do you understand? All the rest we can do without, but of lemons we must needs have a constant supply."

Anne Turner was considerably puzzled to receive this commission, but was even more so when she discovered its hidden meaning. Lemon-juice, it seemed, could be used for writing letters, the writing remaining invisible until you held it over a flame, when the characters would assume a brownish tinge. Mary's captivity was not over-rigorous. From the aged Sister Jacoba Brunnhuberin, who could read the secrets of the heart, the Abbess had learnt that her prisoner in reality was a great servant of God. The whole business was exceedingly painful to her, glad as she was to have such a chosen soul beneath her roof, and she did everything in her power to efface the unfavourable impression of the first night. The community of course, was unable to exchange a single word with the prisoners, and the Sisters were too poor themselves to procure comforts for them; but a message was dispatched to the Paradeiser Haus asking the Sisters to send over the bedding of their Reverend Mother. And every day a large vessel containing little dishes of special food for the invalid was brought and silently deposited on the threshold of her cell. Anne Turner begged the favour of some lemons for a healing draught that had to be prepared with honey and milk for Mary's cough, and thus a brisk interchange of correspondence began on every little scrap of paper that came from the Wein-strasse, all of which, in accordance with the spirit of conventual thrift, were neatly folded and replaced in the basket.

The great moment of the day arrived when the notes thus received were held of a night over the flame of their tallow candle, for all the letters that otherwise reached her, had first to be submitted to the Dean. And at the Paradeiser Haus they lived for the crumpled, greasy little scraps of paper that were read aloud of an evening by Mary Poyntz and Elizabeth Cotton and which were afterwards carefully locked away in a special casket. Their Mother was cheerful and of good courage, they told the community amidst many tears. She was now in a cloister and closed up, she trowed, but the Sisters were kind to her, the Abbess regarding her almost in the light of a daughter, since she, too, had once worn the habit of St. Clare. They were to wait on her (the Abbess), if possible every other day, in all courtesy, reverence, and gratitude, and they were to see that on one such occasion she received a fair silver image as a gift.

To feel grateful over and above all this, thought Mary Poyntz, was expecting rather too much. The very sight of a religious habit, even at the altar, had become almost more than she could endure . . . but, of course, Eliza-beth was right, their Mother would scarce be edified, did she but know of such rebellious thoughts. If only they could do something more for her than send her gingerbread, and sticking plaster, and even that beautiful book of litanies.

To make matters worse, Anne Turner had contrived to add a secret message that Mary's health was suffering seriously from her close confinement in that horrible hole, where even a healthy person could scarce manage to live. She was obliged now to keep her bed and appeared to be troubled with a kind of lameness in one hip and a painful eruption on her left arm. At this juncture, the Electress sent over her own physician with instructions to furnish a detailed bulletin to the Paradeiser Haus. He shook his head and looked very grave, but was forced to own that, strangely enough, never had he had so cheerful, not to say, merry a patient, despite so much weakness and bodily suffering.

By now, Mary had thought out a new plan of action and set about dictating it to Anne Turner, softly and circumspectly, but with sparkling eyes.

"Mistress," she admonished her companion, "why this doleful face? It ill beseemeth a religious to be thus faint-hearted. Are we not, even as we are, comfortable enough? You should see the prisons of our English confessors! A few weeks of peace and quiet in this cloister of ours would suit me well enough, but that I have pledged my word on the bones of the saints. I must return to the battle; this can be but a brief respite at best. The Sisters must write to Rome, not, of course, to say that I am well enough where I am, that is merely between ourselves. Nay, let there be recriminations loud enough to make those concerned hold their very ears. Make a martyr of me, an you will; write them a gruesome story, underlining a word here and there to make it the more emphatic; 'twill be all to the good of the cause. Tell them that what has been committed here is a crying outrage calculated to result in the death of one so sick and weak as myself.—And that's true enough, my Jungfrau, for there's not much of me left. May the Pope and the Cardinals ponder that well.—Petition His Holiness to give me leave to plead my own cause again, and publicly to vindicate my honour since my dishonour hath also been publicly noised abroad. . . . The Sisters fear that I shall be dragged off to Rome? Well, that would not kill me either; like the cat in the proverb, I have nine lives, and I'm not sure but that for the good of our cause, it might not be the best possible thing. In the other event, I fail to see what advantage our enemies would gain by it, for had they designs against my life, they could put me out of the way here with far less ado. They know full well that here we are without friends, and so forth. But what matter whether here or there; if God would have me die, I would not live. Tell Mother Elizabeth to send the last circular again to all our houses, otherwise there will be no satisfying the Dean. Mother Margaret Genison in Vienna is to keep in touch with Father Lamormain, Father Lee to act as their intermediary. Mary Poyntz is on no account to allow any cooling-off in our good relations with the Electress. The Court of Munich has earned my profound regard inasmuch as they have not shown by the slightest coldness or reserve towards me any abatement in their usual confidence and esteem, despite the fact that for the past fortnight they have been fully aware that the warrant was out for my arrest. It cannot have been easy for them to keep silent and remain passive onlookers, believing, as it would seem they do, in my innocence."

It was just as though she were still living in the midst of her orphaned community. All the little details of their daily life to her were matters of all-absorbing interest. Whether they still diligently perused the Lives of the Saints? Whether they were not sitting up too late of nights, since that meant a needless expenditure of light and strength? They were to have their seven hours' sleep, and before six and after ten, there were to be no more worshippers kneeling in the crypt. Mother Cecily was to tend her frost-bitten fingers. All were to be of good cheer and unafraid, and were to have confidence in their loving Master.—Fie upon you, craven Rectrice! Wise Rectrice to cry! That every day I am here Mother Rectrice sing a merry ditty. . . . The letters to Rome have been intercepted and must be sent out again without delay. Let Mother Keys keep a vigilant eye on every mail. Once your petition is in the Pope's hands, she must not on any account be niggardly in sending out copies to the Cardinals. Let her above all be prompt, quietly diligent, and zealous in this matter. Prompt and resolute action is our only hope, and having done all we can, then commend our cause to God that He may vouchsafe pardon and light to all. . . . Be on your guard in all that you say here at the Convent; no complaints must be made, either here or elsewhere. . . . Write, too, in the ordinary way, but on no account write anything from which others may be any the wiser. . . . Had yesterday and the day before good fits of my old disease: this morning have them again and yet have abundance of health and strength to spend for my Lord and Master and in His service. . . ."

One deprivation alone was very bitter. They were denied any participation in the Sacraments, even in Holy Mass. Then, suddenly, Mary's illness took a critical turn for the worse. She was not allowed to take any exercise in the open air, and her cell was too small to permit her freedom of movement. She asked to see a doctor, though she was fully aware that she was not going to die and that her work was not yet done. Dr. Dirmer took an extremely serious view of her case, and the community at the Paradeiser Haus stormed the

Elector with petitions to have the sick woman removed
to her own convent, all the Sisters offering to stand
security for her by sharing her imprisonment. But, as
the Dean explained, such an order did not come within
the jurisdiction of the Elector, consequently all that Duke
Maximilian was able to do was to express his sincere
regrets. Nobody, not even a reigning prince, cared to
dally with the Holy Inquisition. Mary had to remain
where she was.

But on the Feast of St. John Damascene, Confessor and
Doctor of the Church, her physician urged that it was
time for her to receive the Last Sacraments, for she had,
in his opinion, but a few more hours to live. The Sisters
practically went on their knees before the aged Dean,
imploring him not to allow their Mother to die like a
heathen or a dog, for, as everyone knew, every ban and
prohibition were abrogated *in extremis*.

The venerable prelate was in no wise lacking in
humanity; he was even conscious of a sneaking regard for
the prisoner, who inspired him with a disturbing, uncomfortable sort of admiration. But he was also a func-
tionary, acting under strict orders from the Holy Office,
and discipline had to be maintained. He was perfectly
within his rights to administer the Last Sacraments to the
dying woman, but before doing so, he felt he had to
have some pledge that she really had made her submission, and documentary evidence was the safest guarantee,
since it could always be produced when required.

With trembling fingers, he drafted a form of declara-
tion. There it stood in black and white: "If ever she
had said or done anything contrary to faith or Holy
Church, she repented her and was sorry for it." As soon
as the paper with her signature was in his hands, he
would come to her with the Blessed Sacrament. He

gave instructions for the message to be delivered without delay, saying that he, in the meantime, would make the necessary preparations.

*   *   *   *   *

It was already growing dark in the cell of misery and pain. Beyond the half walled-up window, the sky gleamed golden-red, yet cool, when the door opened and the Abbess entered the room. A picture of human misery, Mary lay in her bed, the chill of death already stealing through her limbs. She took the proffered paper and perused it in the fast dimming light. Then followed a brief silence.

"Does His Holiness or the Holy Office require this of me?" she then asked.

"No," said the Abbess, "only the Reverend Dean. . . . Otherwise he does not dare to do what you wish."

A smile flitted over the pale face of the sick woman. Mary let the paper flutter to the floor and half turned to the wall.

"God forbid," she said, "that to cancel venial sins, which, through God's mercy are all that I have to accuse myself of, I should commit a mortal sin, and cast so great a blot upon so many innocent and deserving persons by saying, 'If I have done or said anything against Holy Church. . . .' Nay, my 'If,' with all that is already acted by my adversaries, would give just cause to the world to believe I suffer justly. . . ."

"But you cannot possibly choose to forego Extreme Unction for a mere matter of form," said the Abbess, almost speechless with horror.

"No, no," said Mary, and her voice suddenly rang out as clear as a bell, even to the corridor, where her guardians were holding their breath, as they listened. "I will cast myself rather on the mercy of Jesus Christ and die without the Sacraments."

She half raised herself, her face twitching with pain. "Anne," she cried, "come hither with pen, paper and ink, if the Dean must have his document." And supported by the arms of the Sister kneeling beside her, she wrote in large unsteady characters the proudest and humblest confession of her deeply wounded innocence: "Never have I done or said anything, either great or small, against His Holiness (to whose holy will I have ever submitted myself and do now offer myself wholly to obey), or the authority of Holy Church. But, on the contrary, my feeble powers and labours have been for twenty-six years entirely, and as far as was possible to me, employed for the honour and service of both, as I hope by the mercy of God, and the benignity of His Holiness, will be manifested in due time and place. Nor would I now for a thousand worlds, do the least thing unfitting the dutiful service of a true Catholic and a most obedient daughter of Holy Church—Turn the page; one moment.—Nevertheless, if that which was at the first allowed and authorized by the Supreme Pontiffs, or Sacred Congregations of Cardinals, in which according to my poor capacity I have desired and sought to serve Holy Church, should be by those to whom the decision of such things belongs, determined to have been in any way repugnant to the duty of a true Christian and to the obedience due to His Holiness, or to Holy Church, I am, and ever shall be, with the help of God's grace, most ready to acknowledge my fault, to ask pardon for the offence, and together with the public dishonour already laid upon me, to offer my poor and brief life in satisfaction of the said sin."

Firmly she signed her name, then sank back on her pillow.

"Doth that not suffice?" she queried. "Tell my Sisters to take this to the Dean, and let him answer for it that I die as I am an he will. I will sign nothing more."

For four full days, the matter remained in abeyance. With closed eyes, utterly inert, Mary dictated the nightly lemon-juice letter: The Sisters were to lodge a protest with the Holy Office that she had been denied the consolation of the Last Sacraments. All the necessary instructions were to be sent to the various Superiors in the event of her demise. It was a Christian duty to make one's testament for the sake of others—she herself knew not what was the will of the Lord in her regard.

Then at last her wish was gratified. Extreme Unction was administered and she received the Holy Viaticum. After that she was borne into the church to take leave of her own children at the choir grille, whilst the tremulous peal of the passing bell raised its doleful plaint in the chill air of the early spring evening.

In the streets, the people stood still and whispered: "The great heretic of the *Anger* is dying, consumed by remorse and mortification of spirit. . . . Stubbornly she refused to sue for pardon, and must now see for herself whither her soul is bound. . . ."

But on the following morning, that indomitable woman opened her eyes with a merry smile, and said to Anne Turner: "I know not what the Lord purposes to do with me, but meseems I feel better."

From that day onward, she visibly gained in health and strength. The fever left her and she knew once more what it was to be free from pain. "All will pass," she wrote home. "Sure my soul and body gain by this bargain."

On the Friday before Palm Sunday, the answer came from Rome. Jubilant, the Sisters arrived at the Convent gate, bearing the Pope's order for her immediate release. He had, as a matter of fact, known nothing of her imprisonment. A messenger also appeared from the Elector and his Consort with a gracious letter of felicitation that Mary perused with a queer little smile. Yes, to congratulate someone who had just escaped death was all very well . . . but it was a very different matter to plunge into the depths to save him.

She expressed a wish to spend Palm Sunday quietly in her cell. I know, she told herself, it is the last breathing-space I shall have before taking up the fight anew. It was on this same day twenty years ago that I left the convent at Gravelines to embark on a dark uncertain future. Oh, that hour of parting in the cell at the gate, when I doffed my veil, and to me it was as though I were tearing the living flesh from my own body! And what is the fate that I must prepare to face to-morrow? Has my path grown lighter since then or is it leading me more and more into a tangled labyrinth of darkness;— "The Lord gave, the Lord has taken away. Blessed be the name of the Lord."

PART IV

MARY was back again in her room at the Paradeiser Haus. The joy of reunion had died down, swiftly and fearfully. A week after her return home, the Bull of Suppression was promulgated for Flanders. The Institute was suppressed, uprooted, abolished; its members were absolved from their vows, their official titles prohibited, the habit was to be put off and never reassumed. The Sisters were to part company, not to dwell in the Colleges or Houses, and never again to meet together to consult on any spiritual or temporal matter. They were at liberty to marry or to enter some other order. . . . In forty days they were to have vacated their houses; all their property, including that acquired by their own efforts, was to be confiscated, and their annual revenues were to be cut off. Winefrid was a prisoner of the Inquisition; the letter to the Liége foundation, in which Mary had surmised that the Decree was the work of some individual enemy acting without authority, had been found in her possession. The others left the cities where they had laboured so long as beggars without a roof to cover their heads. Many were forced to beg their bread from door to door of the parents of the pupils they had taught in happier days.

The Paradeiser Haus was swarming with refugees, new arrivals straggling in with every succeeding day. Every bed was occupied, and the classrooms were as full of straw mattresses as they could hold. Mary appealed to the Court and to all her friends for charitable gifts of money and clothes, for the victims were women of gentle birth, amongst them some who were sick and advanced in years, while others were little more than children.

Whatever books, pictures, and furniture could be sold were realized, and the proceeds distributed amongst the refugees to help them on their way. Some were moving on to Vienna and Pressburg, where the edict had not been promulgated—at least, not as yet—but the majority scattered in all directions, like ants from a demolished ant-heap. Friends maintained an embarrassed silence, whilst enemies openly exulted in their victory. Many of the Sisters had no homes to return to, having become completely estranged from their kinsfolk owing to their choice of the religious vocation. Others found the doors of their relatives closed against them because of the stigma of heresy now attached to their names.

What Mary's thoughts were during those terrible days, none could tell. Her hair beneath the unfamiliar cap she had been obliged to adopt was quite white, and in the shabby brown dress in which she went about her tasks her shoulders were very bowed. Former pupils, when they met her in the streets, hurried past with a shame-faced curtsey, some hardly able to restrain a nervous titter at the strange appearance of the Reverend Mother. In church, the pew in which she knelt would empty itself as though by magic, and she soon refrained from addressing any of the clergy whom she met in the street, after witnessing the painful dilemma of a parish-priest, obviously anxious to get away from her, while a crowd of curious onlookers swiftly gathered around them.

The Court in its turn became increasingly aloof, and the revenues on which they depended suddenly ceased to come in. But many a time about nightfall, a messenger would arrive from the Electress—without livery, to be sure—bringing a few ducats or a basket of bread and meat; and in sooth, they stood in dire need of such charity, for all the money they had had at their disposal had been given to the refugees from Flanders.

One day Mary happened to meet an old beggar-woman in the street who, year in, year out, had received from them her daily basin of soup. She stopped to ask with her kindly smile why they had seen nothing of her of late, and whether she had been ill. But the old crone, with a scared glance in all directions, signed her to keep her distance, and hobbled off as fast as her legs would carry her on seeing a Franciscan friar approaching from the opposite end of the alley. With a faint bitterness in her heart, Mary went her way.

"I'm only surprised that a dumb thing still accepts what we have to give," she said miserably to Mary Poyntz, who was strewing crumbs on the window-sill. But when she saw the swollen red eyes that met hers in startled surprise, she hastened to make amends, saying: "Our honour must be dearer to us than life itself, but to lose both for the love of Jesus is surely of little account."

It was almost with a sense of relief that they saw the city becoming more and more preoccupied with the alarums of war and sensational tales of horror, so that people at last had something else to talk about than the scandalous affair of the English Ladies. The Swedish army was steadily heading for the south. In May, Tilly had stormed the stronghold of Magdeburg, but now the Saxons and the Duke of Brandenburg had joined forces with the King of Sweden. Fugitives kept pouring in with tales of the atrocities perpetrated by the Swedish and Imperial troops—a sheer unending story of fire, slaughter, and pillage, of the cruel tortures and outrages inflicted on peasants and burghers alike, of war levies and misery untold. Thus the little company of shabby elderly ladies leading a secluded life in a practically empty house was soon forgotten. In spite of everything, Mary ached to do something to alleviate the misery they saw around them, even though what they had was barely enough for themselves. But every now and then, some of those who had shunned them in their hour of need would remember the saintly stranger in their midst and in that nightmare wrought by the havoc of war would secretly come to her like Nicodemus of old to seek relief for their over-burdened hearts. And, drawing renewed strength from her kind eyes and the brave smile, that had grown so very patient, not one of them went from her unconsoled.

But there were others, bigoted and envious, who surmised, both privately and publicly, that the English heretics were in part to blame for the wrath of God that was bearing so heavily on hapless Bavaria. Priests refused to hear their confessions; stones and mud were flung under cover of night at their windows; garlands of straw were left on their doorstep, and on one occasion Katharina Köchin was even driven out of church with a resounding box on the ear by an indignant sexton amidst the jeers of a crowd of delighted urchins.

When autumn came, Tilly found the tide beginning to turn against him. At the Battle of the Lech, the Iron General received a mortal wound. In vain Catholic altars were stormed with prayers; even the sanctuary of Altötting, the Elector's last recourse, remained mute and dead.

What a mercy in all our misfortunes, was Mary's reflection after the fall of the Bohemian capital, that nothing came of that Prague foundation. The Sisters at Pressburg were cut off as completely as though they were living on an island, after the last stragglers from the Vienna house had left for Munich; however, there was little cause for any anxiety on their account, as they were under the protecting care of Cardinal Pazmany. Cardinal Khlesl had been dead some time, and the Court of Vienna had other things to occupy their attention. Terrible and mysterious rumours were circulating concerning Generalissimus Waldstein and had already reached the ears of the Court of Munich. The King of Sweden maintained his victorious progress; one after another the Imperial cities were falling—Erfurt, Augsburg, Nuremberg and Ulm, and now his troops were heading straight for Munich.

But to Mary, pouring out her grateful heart in prayer for the sorely pressed Emperor, it seemed that the fall of a loyal city to him could not possibly mean so overwhelming a tragedy as to her the apostasy of a faithless soul.

Had there not been three hundred of them who but a year ago were gathered round her banner? Of many, not as much as a trace remained; but of others—and, alas! how many they were—she had heard that with the habit they had laid aside they had also abandoned their vocation and had been entirely absorbed by the world to which they had returned.

"They were quite within their rights," she would assure the few faithful souls, as they sat together, shivering in the darkness of the drear winter evenings, for all the oil and fat they had at their disposal had to be utilized as food of a kind. "They were quite within their rights; the Church absolved them from their vows."

But in the oppressive silence that followed, she would ask herself again and again: "How is it possible that one who has dedicated herself wholly to God and to His love and service, cannot feel herself bound for ever in her inmost heart? That, for the sake of bread to eat and a roof above her head, she can prove faithless to that sacred compact, that she can allow herself to be forced into a marriage to conciliate her kinsfolk, that she can divide once more her allegiance?" And yet this had been the case with the majority, the majority by far, trained in the novitiate of the Institute, bound by its vows. They had sold their inheritance for a mess of pottage and even felt that they had done quite well for themselves, pitying the folly that deterred others from following their example. How were such things possible? "But if it be not my fault—and I no longer believe that for this I shall be called upon to give an account—then all these houses will always be houses to me, and the desire that I have had to advance others in perfection will not be vain or useless to me. . . ."

*   *   *   *   *

And now it was almost the community of the old days that was assembled around the bare board, the little company that had been the first to follow the call, those who had grown grey in service, together with a few young Englishwomen who were either unable or unwilling to return to their native-country. It was impossible however, to go on living as they were doing, from hand to mouth. All they had to keep body and soul together were the odds and ends that Anna Rörlin managed, with infinite labour and at the risk of her life and her honour, to collect on her daily foraging expeditions in the surrounding villages, for every highroad and hamlet were swarming with soldiers, freebooters, and fugitives. But, to be frank, her foraging had brought in little enough for some time past, whilst nothing was to be had in the city, not even for money. Amongst the Sisters, it was whispered (only, to be sure when their Mother was not present), that it was solely due to her prayers that there was always enough, and even to spare, of the pease and mouldy bread that was all they had to live on.

The Court had fled. None of them knew how much longer they would be allowed to remain at the Paradeiser Haus, nor how long it would be before the coming of the Swedes, who, hitnerto in their winter quarters at Mayence, were gradually swarming out, and were now bearing down, ever more swiftly and relentlessly, in a mighty curve on the Palatinate.

One day, searching for something in the locked casket in which the lemon-juice letters had been piously preserved, Mary came upon the fatal Bull that for some time past she had left untouched, for the very sight of it seemed to sear her heart and bring a stifled cry of anguish to her lips.

"The Institute for above reasons is to be suppressed, extinct, uprooted, and abolished; its members are absolved from their vows, the appellations Prepositress, Visitor, and Rectrice forbidden and their official powers to be declared null and void. The Virgins are at liberty to marry, enter other Orders, or also, under the supervision of the Bishop, to live in the world or in their native-country in accordance with their vows. . . ."

"In the world or in their native-country in accordance with their vows." Mary slowly repeated the words, her head bent low over the document, for of late her eyes had been growing very tired. Long nights of weeping had had their share in this, though the Sisters ascribed her infirmity to advancing age and the bitter privations they had had to endure. "We are forbidden to propagate false doctrine and to meddle in matters unbeseeming to us and above our comprehension. But is there a word in this paper forbidding us evermore to teach little girls to read and write? Is there a single word in the Bull to be interpreted in that sense, my Sisters?"

They stared at one another, completely staggered, for the space of a heart-beat, a wild, fond hope gleaming in their eyes like a light seen from far away. Then Winefrid venturedly timidly: "We are expressly forbidden to live in community or to meet to consult on any matter— even our being together here is not quite in order, and the Dean would be extremely angry if he knew of it."

"Indeed!" retorted Mary Poyntz with some heat. "Well, let him provide us with some other shelter against these troublous times, for each one her own separate quarters, then he can have his will!"

"Wrong!" cried Mary, flashing on them the old triumphant smile that awakened undying memories, and all held their breath in eager expectation of what was to come. "There is another way out, for he who published that final clause is also able to repeal it. We must to Rome, my Sisters. Once more I will cast myself at the feet of the Pope and beg him to permit us to open a house in Rome. . . . Yes, my wise masters, your Bull has demolished all but a single stone, and on that stone I will build up my work anew!"

*   *   *   *   *

And now, for the third time, she found herself once more on the glorious, terrible road to Rome, a woman of fifty, with two Sisters and her devoted serving-man. Swollen with the drifting ice-floes of early spring, the rivers seemed to roar out to her their welcome. The mountains opened the encircling ring of their mighty arms that hold the intruder at bay, and took her to themselves in a brotherly embrace, concealed her tracks from bandits and the rag-tag of the roads, led her pursuers astray or buried them beneath avenging avalanches, guiding her through every peril as though from the shelter of one protecting hand into that of the other, until finally the blossoming plain of Lombardy lay stretched out before her eyes.

How grateful was the cordial, courteous welcome accorded the travellers by old friends in the castles of Tuscany after all the misery of those last days at Munich! Everything was just as in the days when, full of hope and confidence, and armed with letters of introduction from Cardinals and Princes, she had set out on the road for the north.

This time, the dome of St. Peter's seemed to loom on the horizon like a beacon of hope and consolation, and when, at last, she knelt at the feet of the Vicar of Christ and said: "Holy Father, I neither am, nor ever have been a heretic,"—oh, how cruelly that stigma still seared her honour, more cruelly than all else she had endured! —the Pope raised her with paternal benignity, assuring her, "We believe it, we believe it."

And now the *Anger* was forgotten and all that had followed after, and she was stretching out eager arms to embrace the new work that was struggling towards the light. Why should the Pope refuse to allow a little company of devout women and children to live beneath the same roof in his city and thus provide a harbour of refuge for young Englishwomen in need of a home?

"We are glad that they should come," was Urban's reply to her petition, "and we will take them under our protection."

Letters were soon constantly speeding backwards and
forwards across the Alps, compiled in accordance with a
carefully pre-arranged code, for the "Jerusalems" still
had designs on her mail, and great circumspection was
needed if her plan for installing the new "loom", and
"baptistery," was not to be frustrated at the eleventh
hour.

"Yellow silk"—a far prettier and far less dangerous
term than the horrid, crude word "money"—was badly
needed, but everything would come right in time; they
were the servants of a great and omnipotent Master.
And what better name wherewith to sign oneself than
Phyllis, Felice, yea, the "happy one" in very truth.
Abraham must have felt much the same when he was
about to sacrifice his son to the Lord, and the angel
showed him the ram caught in the bushes.

The little house on the Esquiline reminded her strangely
of the old days at St. Omer, before they had settled on a
habit or a rule. There were only a very few Sisters,
and they were addressed as Mistress and wore widow's
weeds. They received into their home the daughters of
English *émigrés*, with whom Rome was then swarming.
For in England the times were now more and more
hopelessly out of joint, and there was none who could
predict what would be the end. The King had now been
reigning for six years without a Parliament; the country
was seething with revolt, and the rats were beginning to
leave the sinking ship.

How often that comparison recurred to Mary's mind,
when more and more of her compatriots, Catholic and
otherwise, assembled in her house to indulge in gloomy
prophecies. Why did they not remain where danger
threatened? Why did they not warn the King? Why

were they not on the spot, forearmed against the evil days to come?—She became conscious of a strange new feeling of unrest. She was getting older and older. The physical resources, on which she had so ruthlessly drawn in the past, were now beginning to fail her. Coughs, fever, stone—what was the good, she asked herself, of going to San Cassiano to take the waters, when she found herself, even there, surrounded by a horde of unsleeping watchers, who officiously reported her every movement to Rome, hemming her in with a network of secrecy and suspicion just as though the sick stranger woman were the moving spirit of some dangerous conspiracy.

However, the energetic intervention of the Pope, to whom once more she trustfully appealed, destroyed the sinister web that was being spun around her. He singled her out for delicate attentions, increased the pension he allowed her, placed a carriage and horses at her disposal, sent her wine from his own table, and his own physician to attend her. All this was extremely gratifying, only something seemed to stick in your throat when the letters came in from the Paradeiser Haus with their tales of the unspeakable misery then reigning in Germany, tales of pestilence, and of the Swedish scourge. . . . Three of their Sisters already lay in the little cemetery of the Poor Clares, and Katharina Köchin had been laid to rest in a common grave.

The "beehives," as they were known under their "alias," had now become charity schools, and the hostility of the people of Munich had already given place to kindlier feelings.

"My dear Win," Mary dictated to her secretary, "Jesus forbid that you should make such children as you teach pay one penny for windows, wood, or anything else. Otherwise follow my poor counsel and let it alone. . . ."

It was impossible to help them either. What the
Roman community did not need for itself found its
way secretly into the homes of the *émigrés* to relieve that
proud and hidden misery that crowded round her,
ashamed of its poverty, and still trying to make a brave
show in the eyes of the world. What bliss it was to be
able to help once more. . . . It was only now that Mary
realized what had made the past winter at Munich so
very dark and desolate.

She was still very weak and had to keep her bed a
good deal. From her window, she could see a golden
autumn with all its shimmering glory of sun-kissed
fruition, and to her it was as though something of that
immense peaceful radiance had found its way to the
inmost recesses of her heart. She had writing materials
brought to her bed. She had ever been wont to keep a
strict account of her soul in the form of a meticulous
record encompassed with iron resolutions. But in that
limpid brightness, in that mellowness that had neither
shadow nor bodily substance, boundless and intangible,
that seemed to gush forth from her inmost being, words
altogether failed her. Far away, deep down in the
depths and lost to sight, were the rickety makeshift
expedients that had served their purpose for the laborious
ascent—the ladders that had broken again and again, the
crumbling brickwork that an iron will had built up and
fitted together, stone by stone. . . . Now she was resting
on the silent mountains of God, and heaven was so close
that it seemed she had but to stretch out her hand to feel
it within her grasp.

"O how well ordered are *Thy* deeds, my Lord God!
Then Thou saidst that justice was the best disposition,
now Thou showest how such justice is to be gotten.

"Then Thou saidst what I should do to satisfy for my

sins, now Thou showest where such satisfaction *is to be done*.

"Then Thou showed I should be saved, now the same with some *addition*.

"Nay, I can write no more. Words are vain and poor. My soul, praise thou the Lord."

But that cloying sweetness from without and within, that light that flowed like honey, that whispering silence in which messages undreamt of before began to find utterance, all these things made her fearful and uneasy.

"All this is nothing for me, my Lord. I have been Thy handmaid, ever Thy handmaid. See how coarsened my hands have grown with grinding toil, my shoulders how bowed. It is too late for me now to learn to wind garlands for Paradise; such things are not for me. Hast Thou no more work for me to do? I'm not really tired yet. Discharge me not from Thy service, my Lord; let me die in harness. This garden that Thou hast given me as a refuge for my old age is lovely in very sooth, but I was not created to be a gardener of tender little plants. Too hard was the school in which Thou didst rear me. . . ."

"I'm ungrateful," she said to Mary Poyntz, who arrived laden with flowers and dainties from Madonna Constanza Barberini. "This soft warm atmosphere is stifling me. Just once before I die I fain would feel a hurricane blowing about my ears again."

And still they came from all sides, all intent on spoiling her. The Court and her high-born friends overwhelmed her with so many kindnesses and attentions, that, like a veritable snow-storm of sweet-scented blossoms, they seemed to rob her of her very breath. It was as though everyone wanted to make amends for all she had suffered. Her health, however, steadily grew worse; she felt as though in some strange manner her strength was ebbing away. Her cheerful serenity gave place to a settled melancholy. When letters began to arrive in quick succession announcing that the little company of the staunch old friends of the past was fast dwindling away, hardly a word was heard to pass her lips.

The Electress in Munich was dead. Father Gerard had passed away at the English College—was it really possible that he was seventy-two years old!—and news came from Vienna of the death of the Emperor Ferdinand. Soon she in her turn, responding to the age-old summons, would be joining them in that life beyond the grave.

But not from this cloying inaction; that would be more than I could endure. My work here on the Continent is finished; the new foundation-stone has been laid; the Holy Father's confidence in us is our tower of strength; the Paradeiser Haus is saved. And now the homeland is calling me. I want to die in England.

*   *   *   *   *

The journey northward was made in stages by litter and by coach, then in a westerly direction by way of Milan and Turin. It was hard to resign oneself in patience, to the many halts they were compelled to make, partly owing to her enfeebled state, but even more to the hospitality lavished on her by noble families and princes of the Church. The longing for home had by now become an imperative call, marching orders with which she was now long familiar, sealed, cryptic, but binding, and brooking no delay. She urged her companions to push forward. The next stage, she knew, must be Spa.

Why Spa? Nobody knew, she herself least of all; all she knew was that this was required of her and that she might not tarry. Nothing must deter her, neither the Alpine winter nor the terrible storm that burst over Mount Cenis, in which the little caravan lost its way, and in which four travellers lost their lives. Thanks to their guide's little dog, they found the trail again, and eventually reached Lyons. On arriving in Paris, they learnt that the remittances of which they stood in urgent need had been delayed. Mary had a serious recurrence of her old malady in an aggravated form. Their journey through the war zone baffled description.

What mad world is this? thought Mary to herself in silent dismay. In Munich we trembled for our lives because of the Swedes, but here is the Cardinal sending his generals against the Habsburgs, sending them to the aid of heretics; Catholics against Catholics. Here the banners of Condé and La Force were pressing forward together with those of Weimar against the Spanish Cardinal Infant, against Colloredo and Gallas, her old acquaintances of Prague and Vienna. Only two years ago, Piccolomini and Jan von Werth were besieging Liége. Would peace never return again? Did all this bode the end of all created things? It was so long since they had had peace, that one seemed able to remember nothing but war. Those who were young heard it spoken of much as the Garden of Eden before the Fall, so legendary and far-away it had now become. The tide of fortune was perpetually turning. Now it was rumoured that Jan von Werth, the great German leader, the bogey with whom French mothers were wont to frighten their children, had been taken prisoner and was being dragged to Paris like a caged lion—the troops that were bringing him, they heard, might even pass them on the road.

Then, in a year's time, everything was different. God had given the world to man to rule as he thought fit, and this was what he had made of it!

Everywhere they went, the fields reeked with blood. The defence of the faith had long ceased to be the main object of the eternal conflict. Or was France defending the Church against her most faithful sons, the Habsburgs of Spain and Vienna, when she made common cause with Lutherans and Reformers? Oh, how could the Cardinal, when the Day of Reckoning came, ever reconcile actions such as these with his sacred calling? The world was aflame from sea to sea, and the dread horsemen of St. John's Revelation rode rough-shod over the tortured quivering earth. None seemed able to check this ceaseless slaughter. And God hid His face from the misery of mankind.

The weeks at Spa passed without much gain for Mary in health and strength. She could not even find the time to nurse herself, for an old lady of noble birth, afflicted with a dread disease, clung to her like a leech, never leaving her a moment to herself. But when this stranger, who had lived so long at enmity with God, passed away peacefully, reconciled with her Maker, released at last from so much agony of body and soul, Mary believed that she now understood why she had been uprooted from her quiet life in Rome and sent post haste to Spa. . . . God's ways were not our ways; His designs not ours.

The downfall of a soul thundered louder in His ears than the fall of the stronghold of Breisach, which to men meant lamentation or rejoicing, as the case might be. That one errant soul regained His peace was of far greater moment than all the weighty cogitations and solemn pledges of diplomats in Paris, Rome, or Brussels, in

Munich and Vienna. What was great and what of little account? The soldier had to march whither he was led by the call of the drum. And in the spiritual struggle, it was just the same, no more and no less. The two camps faced each other, armed for the fray, their rival banners fluttering in the breeze. Ensconced in his Babylonian fastness, Lucifer let loose his myrmidons like so many firebrands, whilst on the Mount of the Beatitudes stood Our Lord recruiting His warriors and His disciples. . . . How often she had gazed on that picture in the course of her spiritual exercises! Now it haunted her continually, when she saw the endless columns marching along the dusty or sodden roads, the plumes on the horsemen's hats nodding in the breeze, great banners proudly borne aloft by youthful ensigns, and, as the dominant note, the eternal beating and rolling of the drums. The world was full of anguish; the world was full of the din of battle. How find it in one's heart to bask in the sunlight of an Indian summer in the peace of a sheltered garden?

Her next move was on to Liége. There she found things far worse than even she had anticipated. Many who had once been her own Sisters were still living in the town. Pitiful, indeed, was their bodily plight, but infinitely more terrible the desolation wrought in their souls. With cruel words and bitter taunts they heaped reproaches on the woman whom it pleased them to hold responsible for all their misfortunes. It was almost as though they found a certain vindictive pleasure in revealing thus to her the misery of souls ravaged with hatred and despair. The Sisters who accompanied her were amazed at the patience and calmness with which she listened to one and all. What was there, she asked herself, to be amazed about? "It is part of my atonement,

R

nothing more. For much I *was* to blame. Who but I should suffer and excuse their faults?"

At St. Omer they awaited the arrival of the ship that was to take them back to England. How those days of the long dead past came back to her as, leaning on her stick and the trusty arm of Mary Poyntz, she roamed through the familiar streets of her old begging rounds in the habit of the Poor Clares. . . . O, gateway of the English College, where fate, nay, rather God's inscrutable Providence, roused me from my childhood's dreams. . . . O, cloud of memories, soaring and circling like birds of passage o'er the barren storm-swept garden of my life. . . . It was again the month of May, just as when, as a child, she had set foot for the first time on Catholic soil; May, as in the year when, on the Feast of St. Athanasius, God had summoned her to leave the shelter of the warm nest she had built to be her refuge from the storm.

She sought out the English Convent of the Poor Clares. —was it really thirty years since Bishop Blaise, God rest his soul, had installed them in their enclosure, thirty years since her second clothing and since the day when she had said farewell to her little room beside the wicket, a farewell that it still wrung her heart to recall. She asked permission to see some of the old Sisters who had taken the veil with her at the parlour grille. They hardly knew her again, and conversation soon became difficult, petering out in long, awkward silences. Alas, it was all so very long ago; life for her had been nothing but unrest, whilst for those others behind their consecrated walls it had just meant following the straight path to God. Possibly, too, some dark rumour of Papal Bull and Inquisition had reached also their ears; the disturbances at Liége seemed to have had their repercussions in some totally unexpected quarters. In an unsteady voice, Mary asked to be remembered in their sisterly prayers, then left them, but her eyes were dark with tears.

Was it her own fond yearning, born of unspeakable weariness, or was it a consolation from on high that in the course of a sleepless night, she seemed to hear a voice that said: "Be constant, death is drawing nigh, and great will be your reward." The next morning, she awoke with a heart at peace, even though it was still heavy within her, and the remembrance of some great glory revealed remained with her like the warmth that lingers in a wall after the sun has set.

Beloved grey sea, white cliffs slowly emerging from the mists—dear earth that bore me, that draws me back to her again, as the incoming wave is drawn towards the shore. On the Feast of St. Bernardine of Siena, she was back again in London. Seventeen years was a long time. Dead or vanished from the scene were the friends and companions of the years gone by; young faces, unknown faces, a strange mingling of features familiar and yet unfamiliar, bore the old familiar names. . . . But the yellow waters of the Thames roared beneath London Bridge as of yore; the Tower still loomed massive and sinister; the stairs still led down to the river, whilst gaily decked barges laden with powdered ladies and gentlemen with long curling locks drifted along past its banks. Many more armed men seemed to be about the streets than in former days, strange-looking men in black garments and with closely cropped hair. The Court, to all appearances, had fallen upon evil times, or rather what remained of the Court, for the King was in Scotland. God grant that the war he was waging against those sinister rebels, the Covenanters, ended in victory!

A small community of the Sisters of the Institute was

R*

living near Somerset House under the protection of the
French Embassy on land that had been the marriage por-
tion of the Queen. Strange faces, every one of them;
the youngest Sister was not born when Mary was last
in England. . . . But there, at least, thank God, the old
spirit still lived on. Lived on in spite of Liége and
the Papal Bull and the perfidy of so many. . . . There
the old breed still persisted in young folk, unwearied as
yet and unbroken in body and spirit, who still blithely
sallied forth on the great adventure with the light of
battle in their eyes, went out to meet danger as though
to a feast, and could still laugh loud and heartily when
they talked of threatening letters and house searches.
They donned their bewildering changes of costume
almost, as one might say, for the sheer fun of the thing:
to them a masquerade still spelt Carnival, not the Dance
of Death.

Mary was almost astonished, so completely had she
forgotten that, as far as appearances went, this house
looked much like any other aristocratic residence, and
that the Sisters were accustomed to move abroad in all
the finery of fans and trains and Vandyck lace collars—
so much had she become inured to her life of bitter
penury. Laughingly she shook her head when they tried
to induce her to adopt some similar disguise.

"I'm too old for such things," she said, "and I am well
content, fair ladies, to pass as the faithful old
retainer in charge of your cats."

And with a shy movement that was almost a caress,
her hand softly smoothed the poor russet gown, with its
many darns and patches, that had once been the charitable
gift of one of the Electress's waiting-women in far-away
Munich.

St. Clare, see, I am still your daughter, and not alto-

gether faithless, since I have remained loyal to your liege
and mine, our noble Lady Poverty.

She had no idea that visitors were always inquiring
who was the striking aristocratic-looking old lady
who was now a member of the community, and that
there were even some who were scandalized, so much
did her carriage and bearing appear above her ostensible
station. It was thus that Mary Poyntz suddenly realized
for the first time what truly regal dignity was hers, which
in itself seemed something almost miraculous in such a
beggarly garb. Only, of course, it would never have
done to say as much to their Mother.

Masses were still said daily in the sumptuous private
chapel, and priests still passed in and out, not even very
carefully disguised, either. Archbishop Laud, it was said,
evinced a strange partiality for the old faith, and at Court,
Catholics were even singled out for special attentions.
The Nuncio, Count Rosetti, frequently visited the little
community; the quality entrusted them with the education of their daughters, and a charity school had also been
opened and was being well attended. And all this work
was being carried on very much as a matter of course.

Then, suddenly, the wind veered round to another
quarter, and every few days they were being pestered
with domiciliary visits, one of the consequences, they
assumed amongst themselves, of the eternal Parliamentary broils. Every now and then, the sky would clear
again, only for the storm clouds to gather anew more
threateningly than ever. The King shifted and shuffled
and compromised himself, and it was even rumoured
that the Scots were openly negotiating with the terrible
Cardinal of France.

Then there came a day when Mary knelt weeping in
the chapel, her mind reverting with a cold chill of horror

to that long-forgotten Christmas at Feldkirch. The King
had abandoned Strafford to his fate, and soon after had
come the news of his execution.

How could the King possibly stoop to save himself
by sacrificing the life of his most faithful servant! In
acting thus, he had sealed his own fate, for this world at
least. O God grant that this craven action of his did not
prove decisive for all eternity!

For the first time since her return to England, Mary's
thoughts turned once more to Rome, for the very soil
of the country in which such a crime had been committed seemed to burn beneath her feet. But she refused
to be numbered amongst those who deserted the sinking
ship. The perfidy of the captain, after all, did not
absolve the crew from their allegiance. And in the
sight of God there was always that great, immensely
consoling mystery of atonement.

The autumn brought the news of the Irish rising with
the stories of the terrible slaughter it had brought in its
train. The old fury against the Catholics blazed up once
more. The Nuncio had long been forced to leave the
country. The Queen had gone to Holland, and nobody
believed that her daughter's betrothal was the true reason.
It was rumoured that she had taken the Crown Jewels
with her to levy recruits and raise munitions, and that a
military alliance was being contemplated with the Prince
of Orange. Charles moved to the north, and his departure was a signal for the Catholics, in fact for all the
Royalists, to follow him in a body. Reports were already
beginning to come in of sharp skirmishes in Yorkshire.

There was no remaining in London now. Three big
coaches drew up one day before the little garden adjoining Somerset House, and were soon rumbling along the

great highroad to the north. Big girls and little girls peered out of the windows, whilst among the armed horsemen who acted as their escort was a priest from St. Omer (still sending its legions of death to England), and in the valise of the old serving-man Robert, who brought up the rear, chalice and paten were securely stowed away as in days of old.

In the homes of their kinsfolk in the north, Hutton Rudby, Studley Royal and Ripley Castle, their big family found a refuge for weeks by turns. They were all within easy distance of the haunts of Mary's childhood, and one day she drove over to Newby and Babthorpe.

Strange to be making pilgrimage to the scenes of one's youth as though to a sanctuary. For that was precisely how it seemed to Mary and, like Moses, she fain would have loosened her shoes on the spot where Our Lord had first spoken to her heart: I am what I am.

There, too, she found some few aged servants of her father's, who talked to her of Sir Marmaduke and Lady Ursula, and who knew far more about her sisters than she did herself. Again, as through a veil, she seemed to see her grandparents. Thick with dust hung the lamp in whose faint glimmer the child, lying awake in her bed, had watched the old lady rapt in prayer. Even the beautiful picture of the Blessed Virgin and her little Son, the Baptist and the pear, was still in existence, though much faded and stowed away in some forgotten corner. To Mary it seemed but yesterday, and yet at the same time, very far off and unreal, when she recalled that it was before that same picture that she had learnt to say the rosary and recite her psalter. Strangers had been living at Babthorpe Park for some years past. The new owners received her with every courtesy and, with delicate tact, left her to be alone with her thoughts.

The park had been allowed to run wild. Mightier than ever loomed its ancient trees. Rank grass stood where once smooth lawns had been, and every path rustled with the brittle gold, brown and purple of autumn foliage. Everywhere, the smell of withered leaves seemed to mingle with the fragrance of the past.

Oh, scenes of first love, could anything ever rob you of your enchantment? In the chapel—how small and cramped it struck her now, but, of course, in those days, she had known no other—the black and gold altar still stood as of old beneath the Gothic arch. Other hands were ministering there now; again it was a young girl, as young as she had been in those days gone by. Intimately, tenderly, she handled the beloved old things, and Mary watched her with an odd little pang in her heart, and at the same time with a kind of solemn exultation. Ever anew the torch was being kindled as in the days when she had groped her way alone along the paths of the spiritual life and had sat at old Margaret's feet. In the linen room the same cushions were still lying on the window-seat. How often in that quiet room had she dreamt of a life secluded from the world in the silence of some austere monastic house, of a peaceful cloister with a fountain in the centre bordered with crimson roses. And how different it had been in reality!

She drove over to Hutton with Robert Wright riding behind the carriage. He, too, was revisiting the dead past of his youth. Silent he sat amongst the retainers at the great table in the servants' hall, stood there hat in hand when his brother-in-law, the Squire, passed through, and, as in the quaint old legend of St. Alexis, none recognized in the taciturn grey-haired serving-man the young page who twenty-six years ago had crossed the seas and never been heard of again. And between the two old friends there passed a smile of quiet understanding when Robert respectfully assisted his mistress to alight on the threshold of the stranger house that had become their harbour of refuge from the storm, though neither said a word. They no longer had need of words.

On the Feast of the Exaltation of the Cross, Mary, together with her Sisters and the children, moved to an old house amongst the woods of Hutton Rudby. It stood all alone in the valley; but few folk, and those very poor, lived in the smoke-blackened huts around, whilst within easy distance stood the deserted Carthusian monastery of Mount Grace.

Slowly the great arch was closing of the last forty years.

The trees around the old convent whispered and were hushed into silence. For miles around, the woods blazed brown, yellow, and golden-red, but it was only with the warm glow of autumn tints, not with any reflection of the great Civil strife that was ravaging the land. The din of battle from Edgehill and Brentford penetrated no more to their beech-hidden sanctuary than in other days the destruction of the Armada to the blue nursery of Mary's childhood.

One day, a troop of Roundhead stragglers lost their way in the valley, but what followed might have come straight out of the pages of some faery legend. A young officer, who, despite his close-cropped head, might well have been a knight of King Arthur in disguise, knocked at their door early one morning, and marvelled greatly when, instead of being nearly deafened by women's shrieks, he was greeted by the silvery voices of some hidden choir. A tall white-haired woman, with the bearing of a queen, conducted him with grave courtesy over the house, still to the accompaniment of that

invisible choir of little maidens' voices, until he no
longer knew on what errand he had come, felt unspeakably awkward and uncouth, declined an invitation to
break his fast, and hurriedly rode away along the path
bordered by blue-grey beech trunks back to the valley
where his men were gloomily wiling away the time
with the singing of psalms. And to their inquiries he
vouchsafed no answer whatever, being not quite sure
himself whether by some strange chance he had not found
his way into an elfin dwelling, though the very thought
savoured of superstition. After all, he told himself, no
good could possibly come of riding through the woods
on a misty moonlight night, lured on by twinkling lights
and the sound of distant singing.

Fugitives, too, sometimes knocked at their door, or
the half-starved folk of the surrounding valleys. They
were the guests honoured above all others. Mary invariably insisted on waiting on them herself, and never
would she tolerate their being served with two different
dishes on the selfsame platter. Had not her father in his
day treated his poor with a like consideration? So much,
under the spell of her childhood memories was she,
re-living those days of the past. No beggar was ever
allowed to go away empty-handed; there was always
something still to be found tucked away in odd corners
of chests and coffers, providing you searched long
enough. . . . Why should she hoard things she would
never need again?

Finally she, in her turn, was caught up in the rising
spate of war. So entirely were they now cut off from
any communication with London, that at last with heavy
hearts they decided to move on to York. They found
the city swarming with Royalists, rallying there to make
a last stand for the King, hoping against hope, for the

clansmen were marching across the Border to join forces with the Parliamentary troops. London had fallen; the enemy was already encamped before Oxford, and Henri IV's high-spirited daughter had fled the country in the humble garb of a peasant.

Mary rented a house in the village of Heworth, a mile outside the city, then absorbed in its preparations for a long siege. The life of the little community resumed its normal course—what, indeed, was to be gained by any change in their daily round just because the enemy happened to be on the march; nothing they could do would be able to hold them back.

But in April, Sir Thomas Fairfax routed the Cavaliers at Selby, and shortly after, Cromwell and his men were lying before York. The entire population of the surrounding districts were soon pouring within the shelter of the city's strong walls.

Mary would fain have remained where she was, for she dreaded the confinement and sufferings of a protracted siege far more than open danger. "We will place St. Joseph at one end of the village and oppose the power of the Sacred Name of Jesus to the great cannon and pieces which will keep them from hurting," she said, half laughing, half in earnest.

But, as time went on, the sight of her companions' terror was more than she could endure. Manchester's troops were already on the roads between Heworth and York, and not a single horse or vehicle of any kind was allowed to pass. All their worldly belongings, even their beds, had to be carried through on their own backs. But, as of old, on the military highroads of Germany, they came through unharmed, protected by the mysterious spell of the woman, who, cheerful and serene, headed their little band, trudging along leaning on her stick.

In a tiny room of the besieged city, unable to move from her chair, for she found a recumbent position unendurable and the old agonizing pains were recurring more and more frequently, Mary for six long weeks was a tower of strength to innumerable half-distraught, terror-stricken men and women. Of her it was said that she knew not the meaning of fear and that she radiated strength and confidence. "They went to her as dead and lost, full of fears and alarms, but with her they revived and went away equally filled with courage." And, whether by day or by night, one and all had free access to her who needed her help.

"We cannot suffer," Mary admonished her Sisters, "that anyone be lacking in what we are able to give, whether it be in counsel, consolation, or deed."

"But they do not even thank you, and they forget so quickly," said Sister Helen, venturing a timid protest.

"I don't barter my love," said Mary with a smile, "neither for money, nor thanks, nor praise. We must learn to give freely, my daughters—everything else is but trafficking."

After the surrender of the city, they returned to Heworth. They found their lovely garden laid waste, the trees cut down, the lead and iron torn from doors and windows, and the panes all broken, whilst practically every room reeked with the accumulation of the filth left behind by the soldiers and their sick and wounded. The dead had been hastily buried in the garden, and in the July heat, the very air breathed pestilence. But, though quite indistinguishable from the other rooms, the one that had served as the chapel and Mary's own chamber had remained untouched, and, save for an accumulation of dust, were as neat and clean as they had been left. None had entered there, and there was not as much as the mark of a single footprint on the mats. Both rooms seemed to be waiting to receive a guest or prepared for the celebration of some high festival.

Only too well the Sisters knew who it was who was soon to come. Little short of a miracle it seemed to them that their Mother still lived on. She was so ill that they felt it was almost cruel to pray that her life might be prolonged.

"I have much to do not to beg our Lord to take me," she said herself, and that she owned as much was in itself significant and alarmed the Sisters even more than the change they saw in her face. Alas, there was but one thing that seemed almost too hard to bear: ever since the fall of York they had found it impossible to get in touch with a priest. The Roundheads kept continual watch on the house, and the soldiers, born in the country, were only too well acquainted with every secret means of approach.

No letters came through either, and nobody knew what had become of the community in London. Somewhere, letters from Rome must also be awaiting them, letters, too, from the Paradeiser Haus, and it was to be feared that they might easily fall into the wrong hands.

It was now autumn, after a summer rent by battle and by violent storms, and the last remnants of a ruined harvest were being gathered in. Once again, the solemn woods glowed around the devastated villages, until at last they, too, stood bare, for it was now getting on for All Saints and the first snow had already fallen. For the little community it was a time of endless weary waiting. The first thing in the morning, you went down the garden to the gate to see whether no messenger was in sight, and at night you dared not drop to sleep for fear of missing the secret knock at the door. Mary had already given up asking the same eternal question, but

the Sisters knew only too well that strained look in her
eyes every time she gazed past them in the direction of
the door, and the stiffening of her whole frame directly
the slightest movement was heard outside.

Advent came, brief, dark days of falling snow; endless
nights of blustering, ice-cold winds. No, in such weather,
no messenger was likely to come. Mary lay with her
face to the wall, too tired to pray any more that God
would not let her die before she had news of her absent
children. So weak was she that when evening came, she
was no longer able to control her tears at the last prayer,
with which Compline closes: "May the Divine assistance
remain always with us—*et cum fratribus nostris absentibus.*"

Then came an evening when Winefrid Wigmore
gently laid her hand on her arm, and, to her amazement,
Mary saw that her friend was attired in a long dark travelling cloak.

"I'm going to London," Winefrid announced, "to
fetch the mail."

"Your road lies through the two armies," Mary
demurred.

"I know, I know," said Winefrid; "we've passed
through more than a couple of armies in our time,
haven't we, on those lovely journeys of ours to Rome?
And the roads then were a good deal longer than the
one from Heworth to London."

Neither said: "Shall we ever meet again?" Each knew
that it was for love of the other that those words remained
unspoken, and that it was the very tenderness of that love
that made their parting so brief and matter-of-fact.
What, after all, was a parting, even a parting such as this,
when you'd fought side by side for forty long years?

Then, in her peasant's garb and heavy shoes, the old
woman set out on her long journey, with a lay Sister

as her only companion. Strange that Mary still seemed
to see her from her bed in the darkened room—for her
inflamed eyes could no longer endure the light of day
—saw her pass through the snow-covered garden, in
which the tree-stumps stood round and white like the
broken marble columns on the ruin-strewn fields of
Rome; through the dank leafless beech-wood, then on
and on: still she saw the frail little figure in its heavy
mantle, the blue hood framing the bright eyes and the
face still almost childishly smooth and the thin curls on
either side that seemed so imperceptibly to have changed
from flaxen blond to silken white. Strange, so clearly
she had not been able to see anything for a long time
past, and she found herself wondering whether Winefrid
could see her, too. "Now they are walking along the
banks of the Trent," she said to Mary Poyntz, who
watched day and night beside her bed and could not
quite make up her mind whether her Mother was just
delirious or whether she was seeing visions. . . . "Now
they're at Nottingham—at Leicester . . . they've met
friends there. . . . Oh, do not fear, Mary, they will
arrive safely. And Win will be at home, in time to bury
me."

*　　*　　*　　*　　*

"Stir up Thy might, O Lord, and come. . . . Give
ear, O Thou that rulest Israel. . . . Come, O Lord, and
show us Thy face, Thou that sittest upon the cheru-
bim. . . ."

Mary Poyntz was reading the prayers aloud, the
wonderful Antiphons of Advent, and to the dying
woman it was as though never in the whole of her long
life had she known until now what it meant: to wait for

the Lord, for Him Who was to come, hidden beyond human ken. "Behold the Lord shall come and all His saints with Him and there shall be in that day a great light, Alleluia. Also over our land, Alleluia. Come, Lord, come, and delay not."

But try as she would to control it, the voice of Mary Poyntz faltered when she came to the words: "Lift up your gates, O ye princes, and be ye lifted up, O Eternal gates: for the King shall enter in. . . ." And again: "Who shall ascend into the mountain of the Lord; or who shall stand in His holy place? The innocent in hands and clean of heart. . . ." "Come and free us, O Lord God of Hosts, convert us and show Thy face and we shall be saved."

Behold the Lord descends with might and His strength with Him to visit His people in peace. That was spoken for us, too; for us, too, the Prophets have spoken. The Civil War, all the horrors of the Great Rebellion, and the bitter aftermath of schism, were but as the fleeting shadow of a cloud before His face. Christ our King cometh and the kings shall be silent before His face and the heathens shall pray to Him. And the Lord shall reign for ever over all the nations. Thus it is written. As a mother consoleth, so will He console us. The long nights are light and warm with the promise that gushes forth ever more clearly and abundantly from Holy Writ. How was it possible to feel faint-hearted and afraid? Be comforted, ye of little faith, behold the Lord our God cometh. . . .

He was so near, Mary knew, that it seemed a torment and abomination to prolong that miserable bodily life that was naught but pain and loathing, by artificial means, with physics and nourishment of which the only effect was a renewal of almost intolerable pain. But it had to be endured, so that the Sisters should not be deprived of the consolation afforded by her presence before God willed that it should be so. They had deserved well enough of her that she offered up this sacrifice, too, for their sake. He would surely come Who was to come and would not delay. Eternal life is in His hand. Wait for Him, though He tarries, the Lord is nigh. In the morning we shall see His glory.

Christmastide approached and thank God, a priest had come. Almost miraculously he had succeeded in making his way through the cordon of spies keeping watch on the house. In the holy night, the house at Heworth was ablaze with many lights. Muffled to the eyes, men and women groped their way through the darkness across the blue-gleaming snow and tapped at the windows, from which golden threads of light filtered through the closed shutters. The little chapel was too small to hold the crowd of worshippers, many of whom had come from many miles distant, so to-day the white-spread table that was to cradle the holy Mystery stood in the midst of the hall which had been hung with dark garlands of ivy, fir and holly, bright with scarlet berries. And the Sisters sang: "And the Lord spake to me and said: My Son art Thou" and "A Child is born to us and a Son is given to us."

Mary had risen for the ceremony. Her poor tortured body seemed to be sustained by new strength and she attended all three Masses. How that first Christmas in Rome came back to her and that other one at Feldkirch, the night of the tragic vision before the wooden Crib of the German mountain shepherds.

For a time, this improvement seemed to be maintained, and the Sisters were beginning to believe in a miracle. But on the Feast of the holy Bishop and Martyr, St.

Thomas of Canterbury, she was seized during the night with violent pains and a strange sense of chill in her whole body. She knew it to be the sign.

"I will go and offer myself to our dear Lord in the chapel," she said.

After that, her physical powers began to decline in an alarming way. Her body up to her throat became a swollen, shapeless mass. Her eyes were so inflamed that she was practically blind, and she also lost the use of her feet. But her disfigured face still radiated the old indomitable smile.

On New Year's Day, the priest moved on to his next destination. Before he left, Mary begged him to administer Extreme Unction, but smilingly he refused to grant her request, saying that the Lord had still much work for her to do, and that she was not to think of dying yet awhile. The Sisters were of the same opinion. They had seen her only too often on the very brink of the grave to believe that this time it was deadly earnest. Perhaps, too, right down in their secret hearts, they believed her to bear a charmed life and to be above ordinary human laws.

"Patience," said Mary, "I am not to have that happiness, for I know full well there will be no means hereafter."

Then the last terrible night engulfed her. Was it God's punishment that she was to die without the consolation of the Last Sacraments? Was this the atonement for her refusal of that same consolation years ago at Munich? Was God turning His face from her in her last hour, refusing to recognize her as His child? For so many others she had secured the blessing of a happy death, was she herself to die like an outcast? Faced with this final incomprehensible ordeal, she felt her heart contract and grow rigid with fear, cold and dully apathetic. The longing that was never to be stilled was silent, as though in defiance. Was this the last revolt of self-will that, like a deadly frost, was to blight the fruits of a life-time of faithful, devoted service? With the goal in sight, was her path heading straight for the abyss? There was none who could help her, none. The inner light was extinguished; God would send no other messenger. His priest had refused her consolation, and He had suffered that it should be so. And her Sisters, loving and beloved, suspected nothing, nothing . . . as ever.

The leader is always alone, alone to the very end.

A good thing that Winefrid returned on St. Hilary's day, sorrowful and empty-handed, to be sure; nevertheless it was good to have her there, to see her sitting beside the bed with the faithful love of a lifetime shining in her good kind eyes. Impossible, however, to confide even in her, for she would promptly sally forth in wind and weather in quest of a priest, and an expedition of that nature might easily cost her her life. It was she who received Mary's final instructions. Barbara Babthorpe was to be appointed her Vicar.

"I would they were all here," said Mary sadly, gazing at the little company assembled around her bed. Three hundred of them there had been who had once rallied beneath her banner—where were they now?

"O fie, fie, children! What, still look sad! Come let us rather sing and praise God joyfully for all His infinite loving-kindness. *Te Deum laudamus.* . . ."

Sobbing, the Sisters united their voices with hers. Strangely the cadences of the great hymn of praise rose and fell in the sick-room in the cold light of the dawn.

After it was over, Mary lay there for a long time, calm and peaceful, with closed eyes.

"I wanted to talk to you of other things," she said later on, "but I can say no more. I was always putting it off for fear of giving you pain. And that, too, was why I did not send for a priest. . . . God forgive me if I did wrong; it is that which weighs most heavily upon me now. Do you pray for me."

Out of doors, the sun rose like a ball of fire and hovered flaming before the window.

"Be faithful to my work; carry it on. God will assist you; it is no matter the who, but the what; and when God shall enable me to be in place, I will serve you . . . always . . . always . . ."

Could she still feel on her dying lips the crucifix that, touched for a moment by the rising sun, flooded the whole room with its light?

"She is at peace," said Winefrid softly. "Pray for us, dear Mother!"

*   *   *   *   *

Ingram Content Group UK Ltd.
Milton Keynes UK
UKHW022011100423
419954UK00011B/179